Chronological Tables
of American Newspapers

1690 – 1820

Chronological Tables
of American Newspapers
1690-1820

Being a tabular guide to holdings of
newspapers published in America
through the year 1820

COMPILED BY

Edward Connery Lathem

American Antiquarian Society
& Barre Publishers

BARRE · MASSACHUSETTS

INTRODUCTION

THIS VOLUME has been prepared as a companion to Clarence S. Brigham's *History and Bibliography of American Newspapers 1690–1820*, published by the American Antiquarian Society in 1947 and supplemented by a fifty-page compilation of 'Additions and Corrections' which was included in the Society's *Proceedings* for April of 1961 and was issued, also, in separate form. (The two Brigham volumes, plus the supplement, were reprinted in 1962 by Archon Books of Hamden, Connecticut.)

The tables that follow are intended to serve as aids in approaching, on a chronological basis, available issues of American newspapers for the period through 1820. By consulting columns representing the year or years pertinent to a matter under investigation, users can readily determine what papers may exist, either for particular localities or generally, as potentially helpful resources.

Within the tables, dates are entered which indicate each newspaper's span of publication or of its current availability. The words 'from' and 'to' specify that, respectively, the newspaper was initially established on the date given or its publication permanently ceased then and that, moreover, copies are still extant for those dates. Where, however, the coverage of present-day holdings does not begin or end with the actual commencement or conclusion of publication, the terms 'first known' and 'last known' are employed instead. Intervals of suspension have been noted, and when the word 'suspended' appears, the date cited is that of the issue immediately following which a suspension occurred, while 'resumed' identifies the very date when resumption took place. Symbols are provided (√ × ○) to reflect the extent to which, for each year of publication, individual numbers are known to be accessible. No notice is taken herein of issues that formerly existed but are no longer locatable.

After consulting the tables of this volume, appropriate reference should be made to the Brigham bibliography for more detailed information. Thereafter, consultation of the newspapers themselves can be achieved either through application to repositories having actual issues or, alternatively, through the use of existing photo facsimiles, such as those in 'The Microprint Edition of Early American Newspapers 1704–1820,' a series projected by the Readex Microprint Corporation of New York City in association with the American Antiquarian Society. Brigham in his supplement mentions many instances of photocopy provision made by individual libraries or other agencies, but of even greater usefulness in this connection is, of course, *Newspapers on Microfilm*, compiled by George A. Schwegmann Jr. and published by the Library of Congress.

Dartmouth College   E.C.L.
Hanover, New Hampshire
January 1972

NAMES OF NEWSPAPERS REPRESENTED IN THESE TABLES are given in accordance with the form of their entry in Clarence S. Brigham's *History and Bibliography of American Newspapers 1690–1820* and its supplement. It has been necessary, however, to abbreviate particularly long names, in order to accommodate them within the tables' columns. All of the abbreviations used are indicated in the following list, the deleted elements set off by pointed brackets—except that, to conserve space generally, unessential punctuation has been dropped from titles and ampersands occasionally employed in the tables to replace 'and,' without noting here the instances of such.

CONNECTICUT
[New Haven] Conn⟨ecticut⟩ Post, and N⟨ew⟩ H⟨aven⟩ Visitor
New-Haven Gazette, and Conn⟨ecticut⟩ Magazine

DELAWARE
[Wilmington] Del⟨aware⟩ and Eastern-Shore Adv⟨ertiser⟩

DISTRICT OF COLUMBIA
[Georgetown] Museum; Georgetown Adv⟨ertiser⟩
[Georgetown] Times, and Patowmack Pack⟨et⟩
[Washington] American Literary Adv⟨ertiser⟩

GEORGIA
[Petersburg] Georgia & C⟨arolina⟩ Gazette

MARYLAND
[Annapolis] M⟨arylan⟩d Gazette, and Annapolis Adv⟨ertiser⟩
[Baltimore] Edwards's Balt⟨imore⟩ Daily Adv⟨ertiser⟩
[Baltimore] Neue Unpartheyische B⟨altimore⟩ Bote
[Fredericktown] Bartgis's M⟨arylan⟩d Gazette
[Fredericktown] Bartgis's M⟨arylan⟩d⟨ische⟩ Zeitung
[Fredericktown] Bartgis's Republican Gaz⟨ette⟩
[Fredericktown] Independent Amer⟨ican⟩ Vol⟨unteer⟩

NEW HAMPSHIRE
[Dover] Political and Sentimental Repos⟨itory⟩

NEW JERSEY
[New Brunswick] Arnett's Bruns⟨wick⟩ Adv⟨ertiser⟩
[New Brunswick] Arnett's N⟨ew-⟩J⟨ersey⟩ Federalist

[Philadelphia] Penn⟨sylvania⟩ Evening Herald
[Philadelphia] Pensy⟨lvanische⟩ Correspondenz
[Philadelphia] Penn⟨sylvanische⟩ Staats-Courier
[Philadelphia] Political and Commercial Reg⟨ister⟩
[Philadelphia] Poulson's Amer⟨ican⟩ Daily Adv⟨ertiser⟩
[Philadelphia] Relf's Phila⟨delphia⟩ Prices Current
[Philadelphia] Scott's Phila⟨delphia⟩ Price-Current
[Philadelphia] Story & H⟨umphreys⟩'s Penn⟨sylvania⟩ Mercury
[Philadelphia] Wochentliche Phila⟨delphische⟩ Staats⟨bote⟩
[Reading] Neue Unpartheyische R⟨eadinger⟩ Zeit⟨ung⟩
[West Chester] Chester and Del⟨aware⟩ Federalist

RHODE ISLAND
[Providence] Manufacturers' & Farmers' J⟨ournal⟩

SOUTH CAROLINA
[Charleston] Gazette of the State of S⟨outh-⟩C⟨arolina⟩
[Charleston] S⟨outh-⟩C⟨arolina⟩ and American General Gaz⟨ette⟩
[Charleston] S⟨outh-⟩C⟨arolina⟩ Gaz⟨ette⟩; And Country Journal
[Charleston] S⟨outh-⟩C⟨arolina⟩ Gaz⟨ette⟩ and General Adv⟨ertiser⟩
[Charleston] South-Carolina Weekly Adv⟨ertiser⟩
[Charleston] S⟨outh⟩ C⟨arolina⟩ Weekly Chronicle
[Charleston] South-Carolina Weekly Gaz⟨ette⟩
[Charleston] So⟨uthern⟩ Evangelical Intelligencer
[Charleston] State Gaz⟨ette⟩ of South-Carolina
[Georgetown] S⟨outh-⟩C⟨arolina⟩ Independent Gazette

TENNESSEE
[Jonesborough] Newspaper and Wash⟨ington⟩ Adv⟨ertiser⟩

VIRGINIA
[Richmond] V⟨irgini⟩a Gazette, and General Adv⟨ertiser⟩
[Richmond] V⟨irgini⟩a Gazette and Ind⟨ependent⟩ Chronicle
[Richmond] V⟨irgini⟩a Gazette, and Public Adv⟨ertiser⟩
[Richmond] V⟨irgini⟩a Gazette, and R⟨ichmond⟩ and
        M⟨anchester⟩ Adv⟨ertiser⟩
[Richmond] V⟨irgini⟩a Gazette & R⟨ichmond⟩ Chronicle
[Richmond] V⟨irgini⟩a Gazette: and R⟨ichmond⟩ Daily Adv⟨ertiser⟩
[Richmond] V⟨irgini⟩a Gazette, and Weekly Adv⟨ertiser⟩
[Richmond] V⟨irgini⟩a Gazette, or, ⟨the⟩ Amer⟨ican⟩ Adv⟨ertiser⟩

[Richmond] V⟨irgini⟩a Independent Chronicle
[Williamsburg] Virginia Gazette (Dixon ⟨& Nicolson⟩)
[Williamsburg] Virginia Gazette (Hunter⟨, Royle, Purdie & Dixon,
      Dixon & Hunter⟩)
[Williamsburg] Virginia Gazette (Purdie⟨, Clarkson & Davis⟩)
[Williamsburg] Virginia Gazette (Rind⟨, Pinkney⟩)
    WEST VIRGINIA
[Wheeling] V⟨irgini⟩a North-Western Gazette

Chronological Tables
of American Newspapers

1690 – 1820

Chronological Tables of American Newspapers 1690–1820

Tables for 1690–1729

MASSACHUSETTS

	1690	1691	1692	1693	1694	1695	1696	1697	1698	1699
[Boston] Publick Occurrences	first and only issue 25 Sept	·	·	·	·	·	·	·	·	·

MASSACHUSETTS

	1700	1701	1702	1703	1704	1705	1706	1707	1708	1709
Boston News-Letter					from 24 Apr ✓	✓	✓	✓	✓	(suspension) ×

MASSACHUSETTS

	1710	1711	1712	1713	1714	1715	1716	1717	1718	1719
Boston Gazette	·	·	·	·	·	·	·	·	·	from 21 Dec
Boston News-Letter	×	✓	✓	✓	✓	✓	✓	✓	✓	✓

PENNSYLVANIA

	1710	1711	1712	1713	1714	1715	1716	1717	1718	1719
[Philadelphia] American Weekly Mercury	·	·	·	·	·	·	·	·	·	from 22 Dec ✓

MARYLAND

	1720	1721	1722	1723	1724	1725	1726	1727	1728	1729
[Annapolis] Maryland Gazette	·	·	·	·	·	·	·	·	first known 10 Dec ✓	✓

MASSACHUSETTS

	1720	1721	1722	1723	1724	1725	1726	1727	1728	1729
Boston Gazette	✓	✓	✓	✓	✓	✓	last known 25 June ✓			
[Boston] New-England Courant		from 7 Aug ✓	✓	✓	✓	✓				
[Boston] New-England Weekly Journal								from 20 Mar ✓	✓	✓
Boston News-Letter	✓	✓	✓	✓	✓	✓	✓	✓	✓	✓

NEW YORK

	1720	1721	1722	1723	1724	1725	1726	1727	1728	1729
New-York Gazette	·	·	·	·	·	·	first known 7 Mar ✓	✓	✓	✓

PENNSYLVANIA

	1720	1721	1722	1723	1724	1725	1726	1727	1728	1729
[Philadelphia] American Weekly Mercury	✓	✓	✓	✓	✓	✓	✓	✓	✓	✓
[Philadelphia] Pennsylvania Gazette	·	·	·	·	·	·	·	·	from 24 Dec ✓	✓

	1730	1731	1732	1733	1734	1735	1736	1737	1738	1739
MARYLAND										
[Annapolis] Maryland Gazette	×	(suspension) o	(suspension) o	×	last known 29 Nov ×					
MASSACHUSETTS										
Boston Evening-Post						from 18 Aug √	√	√	√	√
Boston Gazette	√	√	√	√	√	√	√	√	√	√
[Boston] New-England Weekly Journal	√	√	√	√	√	√	√	√	√	√
Boston News-Letter	√	√	√	√	suspended 24 Jan; resumed 7 Feb √	√	√	√	√	√
Boston Post-Boy						first known 21 Apr √	√	×	×	√
[Boston] Weekly Rehearsal		from 27 Sept √	√	√	√	to 11 Aug √				
NEW YORK										
New-York Gazette	√	√	√	√	√	√	√	√	√	√
New-York Weekly Journal				from 5 Nov √	√	√	√	√	√	√
PENNSYLVANIA										
[Germantown] Hoch-Deutsch Pensy. Ges.										from 20 Aug ×
[Philadelphia] American Weekly Mercury	√	√	√	√	√	√	√	√	√	√
[Philadelphia] Pennsylvania Gazette	√	√	√	√	√	√	√	√	√	√
Philadelphische Zeitung			first & only other known: 6 May & 24 June							
RHODE ISLAND										
[Newport] Rhode-Island Gazette			first known 4 Oct √	last known 1 Mar √						
SOUTH CAROLINA										
[Charleston] South-Carolina Gazette			from 8 Jan √	suspended 8 Sept √	resumed 2 Feb √	√	√	√	√	√
VIRGINIA								first known 10 Sept √		
[Williamsburg] Virginia Gazette (Parks)							first known 10 Sept √	√	√	√

Page 3   SYMBOLS: √ complete or extensive coverage exists   × few numbers known (usually less than 25 % of those issued)   o no copies extant   Table for 1730–1739

Chronological Tables of American Newspapers 1690–1820

Table for 1740–1749

	1740	1741	1742	1743	1744	1745	1746	1747	1748	1749
MARYLAND										
[Annapolis] Maryland Gazette						first known 26 Apr √	√	√	√	√
MASSACHUSETTS										
Boston Evening-Post	√	√	√	√	√	√	√	√	√	√
Boston Gazette	√	√	√	√	√	√	√	√	√	√
[Boston] Independent Advertiser									from 4 Jan √	suspended 2 Oct; only other issued 5 Dec √
[Boston] New-England Weekly Journal	√	to 13 Oct √								
Boston News-Letter	√	√	√	√	√	√	√	√	√	√
Boston Post-Boy	√	√	√	√	√	√	√	√	√	√
NEW YORK										
New-York Evening-Post					first known 17 Dec √	√	√	√	(suspension) √	√
New-York Gazette	√	×	○	○	last known 29 Oct ×					
New-York Gazette or Weekly Post-Boy								from 19 Jan √	√	√
New-York Weekly Journal	√	√	√	√	√	√	√	√	√	√
New-York Weekly Post-Boy				from 3 Jan √	√	√	√	to 12 Jan √		
PENNSYLVANIA										
[Germantown] Hoch-Deutsch Pensy. Ges.	○	○	×	√	√	√	to 16 May √			
[Germantown] Pensylvanische Berichte							from 16 June √	√	√	√
[Philadelphia] American Weekly Mercury	√	√	√	√	√	√	last known 22 May √			
[Philadelphia] Pennsylvania Gazette	√	√	√	√	√	√	√	√	√	√
[Philadelphia] Pennsylvania Journal			from 2 Dec √	√	√	√	√	√	√	√
SOUTH CAROLINA										
[Charleston] South-Carolina Gazette	√	√	√–	√	√	√	√	√	√	√

Publication	1740	1741	1742	1743	1744	1745	1746	1747	1748	1749	1750	1751	1752	1753	1754	1755	1756	1757	1758	1759
VIRGINIA																				
[Williamsburg] Virginia Gazette (Parks)	×	o	o	o	o	√	last known 25 Sept √		√											
CONNECTICUT																				
[New Haven] Connecticut Gazette												√	√	√	√	from 12 Apr √	√	√	√	√
New-London Summary																			first known 29 Sept √	√
MARYLAND																				
[Annapolis] Maryland Gazette						√	√	√	√	√	√	√	√	√	√	√	√	√	√	√
MASSACHUSETTS																				
Boston Evening-Post	√	√	√	√	√	√	√	√	√	√	√	√	√	√	√	√	√	√	√	√
Boston Gazette	√	√	√	√	√	√	√	√	√	√	√	√	√	√	√	√	√	√	√	√
Boston News-Letter	√	√	√	√	√	√	√	√	√	√	√	√	√	√	√	√	√	√	√	√
Boston Post-Boy	√	√	√	√	√	√	√	√	√	√	√	√	√	√	last known before suspension 23 Dec √			resumed 22 Apr √	√	√
NEW HAMPSHIRE																				
[Portsmouth] New-Hampshire Gazette																	from 7 Oct √	√	√	√
NEW YORK																				
New-York Evening-Post	√	√	last known 18 Dec ×																	
New-York Gazette or Weekly Post-Boy				√	√	√	√	√	√	√	√	√	√	√	√	√	√	√	√	√
New-York Gazette [Weyman's]																				(prospectus issue 16 Feb √) from 19 Feb √
[New York] Independent Reflector													from 30 Nov √	to 22 Nov √						
[New York] Instructor																from 6 Mar; last known 8 May √				
[New York] John Englishman																from 9 Apr; last known 5 July √				
New-York Mercury													first known 31 Aug √	√	√	√	√	√	√	√
[New York] Occasional Reverberator														from 7 Sept to 5 Oct √						

Page 5   SYMBOLS: √ complete or extensive coverage exists   × few numbers known (usually less than 25% of those issued)   o no copies extant

1750–1759

	1750	1751	1752	1753	1754	1755	1756	1757	1758	1759
NEW YORK *continued*										
New-York Weekly Journal	✓	last known 18 Mar ✓								
NORTH CAROLINA										
[New Bern] North-Carolina Gazette		first known 15 Nov ✗	✗	✗	○	○	○	✗	○	last known 18 Oct ✗
PENNSYLVANIA										
[Germantown] Pensylvanische Berichte	✓	✓	✓	✓	✓	✓	✓	✓	✓	✓
Lancastersche Zeitung			first known 29 Jan ✗	last known 5 June ✗						
[Philadelphia] Hoch Teutsche und E. Zeit.				first & only other known: 1 & 25 Jan						
[Philadelphia] Pennsylvania Gazette	✓	✓	✓	✓	✓	✓	✓	✓	✓	✓
[Philadelphia] Pennsylvania Journal	✓	✓	✓	✓	✓	✓	✓	✓	✓	✓
Philadelphische Zeitung						first known 6 Sept ✗	✗	last known 31 Dec ✓		
RHODE ISLAND										
Newport Mercury									from 19 June ✗	✓
SOUTH CAROLINA										
[Charleston] South-Carolina Gazette	✓	✓	✓	✓	✓	✓	✓	✓	✓	✓
[Charleston] South-Carolina Weekly Gaz.										first of two issues known 31 Oct
VIRGINIA										
[Williamsburg] Virginia Gazette (Hunter)	first known 17 Jan ✓	✓	✓	✗	○	✓	✗	✗	○	✗

1760–1769

	1760	1761	1762	1763	1764	1765	1766	1767	1768	1769
CONNECTICUT										
[Hartford] Connecticut Courant					(specimen issue 29 Oct) first known 3 Dec ✓	✓	✓	✓	✓	✓
[New Haven] Connecticut Gazette		✓	✓	✓	suspended 14 Apr ✓	resumed 5 July ✓	✓	✓	to 19 Feb ✓	
[New Haven] Connecticut Journal								from 23 Oct ✓	✓	✓
[New London] Connecticut Gazette				from 18 Nov ✓	✓	✓	✓	✓	✓	✓

	1760	1761	1762	1763	1764	1765	1766	1767	1768	1769
CONNECTICUT continued										
New-London Summary	✓	✓	✓	last known 23 Sept ✓						
GEORGIA										
[Savannah] Georgia Gazette				from 7 Apr ✓	✓	suspended 21 Nov ✓	resumed 21 May ✓	✓	✓	✓
MARYLAND										
[Annapolis] Maryland Gazette	✓	✓	✓	✓	✓	(suspension) ✓	(suspension) ✓	✓	✓	✓
MASSACHUSETTS										
Boston Chronicle								from 21 Dec ✓	✓	✓
Boston Evening-Post	✓	✓	✓	✓	✓	✓	✓	✓	✓	✓
Boston Gazette	✓	✓	✓	✓	✓	✓	✓	✓	✓	✓
[Boston] Massachusetts Gazette									from 23 May ✓	to 25 Sept ✓
Boston News-Letter	✓	✓	✓	✓	✓	✓	✓	✓	✓	✓
Boston Post-Boy	✓	✓	✓	✓	✓	✓	✓	✓	✓	✓
[Salem] Essex Gazette									from 2 Aug ✓	✓
NEW HAMPSHIRE										
Portsmouth Mercury						from 21 Jan ✓	last known 29 Sept ✓			
[Portsmouth] New-Hampshire Gazette	✓	✓	✓	✓	✓	✓	✓	✓	✓	✓
NEW JERSEY										
[Woodbridge] Constitutional Courant						only known 21 Sept				
NEW YORK										
[New York] American Chronicle			from 20 Mar; last known 22 July ✓							
New-York Chronicle										from 8 May ✓
New-York Gazette or Weekly Post-Boy	✓	✓	✓	✓	✓	✓	✓	✓	✓	✓
New-York Gazette [Weyman's]	✓	✓	✓	✓	✓	(suspension) ✓	✓	to Dec 28 ✓		

Page 7   SYMBOLS: √ complete or extensive coverage exists   × few numbers known (usually less than 25% of those issued)   o no copies extant   Table for 1760–1769

Chronological Tables of American Newspapers 1690–1820

	1760	1761	1762	1763	1764	1765	1766	1767	1768	1769
NEW YORK continued										
New-York Gazette and Weekly Mercury									from 1 Feb √	√
New-York Journal							from 16 Oct √	√	√	√
New-York Mercury	√	√	√	√	√	√	√	√	to 25 Jan √	
New-York Pacquet				prelim. issue 11 July; other known 22 Aug.						
NORTH CAROLINA										
[New Bern] North-Carolina Gazette									first known 24 June ×	(suspension?) ×
[New Bern] North Carolina Magazine					first known 6 July √	last known 18 Jan √				
[Wilmington] Cape-Fear Mercury										first known 24 Nov ×
[Wilmington] North-Carolina Gazette						first known 20 Nov (extra) √	last known 26 Feb √			
PENNSYLVANIA										
[Germantown] Pensylvanische Berichte	√	√	last known 26 Aug √							
[Germantown] Wahre und W. Begeben.							only known 24 Feb			
Germantowner Zeitung				first known 15 Dec ×	o	o	×	o	×	o
[Philadelphia] Pennsylvania Chronicle								from 26 Jan √	√	√
[Philadelphia] Pennsylvania Gazette	√	√	√	√	√	(suspension in Nov) √	√	√	√	√
[Philadelphia] Pennsylvania Journal	√	√	√	√	√	√	√	√	√	√
[Philadelphia] Penny Post										from 9 Jan; last known 27 Jan √
[Philadelphia] Wochentliche Phila. Staats.			from 18 Jan √	√	√	√	√	√	√	√
RHODE ISLAND										
Newport Mercury	×	×	√	√	√	√	√	√	√	√
Providence Gazette			from 20 Oct √	√	√	suspended 11 May (extra 24 Aug) √	(extra & supplem't 12 Mar) res. 9 Aug √	√	√	√
SOUTH CAROLINA										
[Charleston] S.C. & American General Gaz.					first known 18 Apr (supplement) ×	×	√	√	√	√

SOUTH CAROLINA continued

	1760	1761	1762	1763	1764	1765	1766	1767	1768	1769
[Charleston] South-Carolina Gazette	✓	✓	✓	✓	susp. 31 Mar (except 25 Aug) res. 1 Oct ✓	suspended 31 Oct ✓	resumed 2 June ✓	✓	✓	✓
[Charleston] S.C. Gaz. & Country Journal						from 17 Dec ✓	✓	✓	✓	✓
[Charleston] South-Carolina Weekly Gaz.	other of two issues known 10 Dec									
VIRGINIA										
[Williamsburg] Virginia Gazette (Hunter)	○	×	×	×	○	× (suspension)	first after suspension 7 Mar ✓	✓	✓	✓
[Williamsburg] Virginia Gazette (Rind)							from 16 May ✓	×	✓	✓

	1770	1771	1772	1773	1774	1775	1776	1777	1778	1779
CONNECTICUT										
[Hartford] Connecticut Courant	✓	✓	✓	✓	✓	✓	✓	✓	✓	✓
[New Haven] Connecticut Journal	✓	✓	✓	✓	✓	✓	✓	✓	✓	✓
[New London] Connecticut Gazette	✓	✓	✓	✓	✓	✓	✓	✓	✓	✓
Norwich Packet				first known 4 Nov ✓	✓	✓	✓	✓	✓	✓
GEORGIA										
[Savannah] Georgia Gazette	✓	○	×	×	✓	✓	last known 7 Feb ✓			
[Savannah] Royal Georgia Gazette										first known 11 Feb ×
MARYLAND										
[Annapolis] Maryland Gazette	✓	✓	✓	✓	✓	✓	✓	suspended 25 Dec ✓	✓	resumed 30 Apr ✓
[Annapolis] Md. Gazette & Annapolis Adv.										first & only other known: 9 & 23 July
[Baltimore] Dunlap's Maryland Gazette						from 2 May ✓	✓	✓	to 8 Sept ✓	
[Baltimore] Maryland Gazette									from 15 Sept ✓	last known before suspension 5 Jan
[Baltimore] Maryland Journal				from 20 Aug ✓	✓	✓	✓	✓	✓	✓
MASSACHUSETTS										
[Boston] American Gazette									only known 2 Apr	

SYMBOLS: ✓ complete or extensive coverage exists × few numbers known (usually less than 25% of those issued) ○ no copies extant

Tables for 1760–1779

Chronological Tables of American Newspapers 1690–1779

Table for 1770–1779

MASSACHUSETTS continued	1770	1771	1772	1773	1774	1775	1776	1777	1778	1779
[Boston] Censor		from 23 Nov √	last known 2 May √							
Boston Chronicle	to 25 June √									
[Boston] Continental Journal							from 30 May √	√	√	√
Boston Evening-Post	√	√	√	√	√	to 24 Apr √				
[Boston] Evening Post									from 17 Oct √	√
Boston Gazette	√	√	√	√	√	suspended 17 Apr; resumed 5 June √	√	√	√	√
[Boston] Independent Chronicle							from 19 Sept √	√	√	√
[Boston] Independent Ledger									from 15 June √	√
[Boston] Massachusetts Spy	from 17 July √	suspended 1 Feb; resumed 7 Mar √	√	√	√	to 6 Apr √				
[Boston] New-England Chronicle							from 25 Apr; to 12 Sept √			
Boston News-Letter		√	√	√	√	last known 17 Apr √	last known 22 Feb √			
Boston Post-Boy	√	√	√	√	√	last known 17 Apr √				
[Cambridge] New-England Chronicle						from 12 May √	to 4 Apr √			
[Newburyport] Essex Journal				from 4 Dec √	√	(except 14 July) √	√	to 13 Feb √		
[Salem] American Gazette							from 12 June; last known 30 July √			
[Salem] Essex Gazette	√	√	√	√	√	to 2 May √				
Salem Gazette					(prospectus issue 24 June) from 1 July √	last known 21 Apr √				
[Worcester] Massachusetts Spy						from 3 May √	(suspensions in Feb–May) √	√	√	√
NEW HAMPSHIRE										
Exeter Journal									first known 24 Feb √	to 25 May √
[Exeter] New Hampshire Gazette							(prospectus issue 22 May) from 1 June √	last known 15 July √		
[Hanover] Dresden Mercury										first & last known: 13 July √ & 27 Sept √
[Portsmouth] Freeman's Journal							from 25 May √	√	to 9 June √	

NEW HAMPSHIRE continued	1770	1771	1772	1773	1774	1775	1776	1777	1778	1779
[Portsmouth] New-Hampshire Gazette	√	√	√	√	√	(except 24 Oct) √	suspended 9 Jan(?) √		resumed 16 June √	√
NEW JERSEY										
[Bridgeton] Plain Dealer						from 25 Dec √	to 12 Feb √			
[Burlington] New-Jersey Gazette								from 5 Dec √	to 25 Feb √	
[Chatham] New-Jersey Journal										from 16 Feb √
[Newark] New-York Gazette							from 21 Sept to 2 Nov √			
[Trenton] New-Jersey Gazette									from 4 Mar √	(except 7, 14 & 21 July) √
NEW YORK										
Albany Gazette		from 25 Nov √	last known 3 Aug √							
[Fishkill] New-York Packet								first known 6 Feb √	√	√
[Kingston] New York Journal								from 7 July to 13 Oct √		
New-York Chronicle	last known 4 Jan √									
[New York] Constitutional Gazette						first known 9 Aug √	last known 28 Aug √			
New-York Gazette or Weekly Post-Boy		√	√	last known 12 July √						
New-York Gazette and Weekly Mercury	√	√	√	√	√	√	√	√	√	
New-York Journal	√	√	√	√	√	√	to 29 Aug √			
New-York Mercury										first known 10 Sept √
New York Packet							from 4 Jan to 29 Aug √			
[New York] Rivington's N.Y. Gazette								from 4 Oct; only other known 11 Oct		
[New York] Rivington's N.Y. Gazetteer				from 22 Apr (preliminary issue 18 Mar) √	√	to 23 Nov √				
[New York] Rivington's N.Y. Loyal Gaz.								from 18 Oct to 6 Dec √		
[New York] Royal American Gazette								from 16 Jan √	√	√
[New York] Royal Gazette								from 13 Dec √	√	√

Page II   SYMBOLS: √ complete or extensive coverage exists   x few numbers known (usually less than 25% of those issued)   o no copies extant   Table for 1770–1779

Chronological Tables of American Newspapers 1690–1820

Table for 1770–1779

	1770	1771	1772	1773	1774	1775	1776	1777	1778	1779
NEW YORK continued										
[Poughkeepsie] New-York Journal									from 11 May √	√
NORTH CAROLINA										
[New Bern] North-Carolina Gazette	○	○	○	×	×	√	(suspension?) ○	√		
[Wilmington] Cape-Fear Mercury	×	○	○	×	(suspension) ×	last known 1 Sept ×				
PENNSYLVANIA										
Germantowner Zeitung	○	×	○	×	×	×	×	last known 19 Mar ×		
Lancaster Mercury										only known supplement of ca. 1 Apr
[Lancaster] Pennsylvania Packet								from 29 Nov √	to 17 June √	√
[Lancaster] Pennsylvanische Zeitungs-Blat									from 4 Feb to 24 June √	
[Philadelphia] Pennsylvania Chronicle	√	√	√	√	to 8 Feb √					
[Philadelphia] Pennsylvania Evening Post						from 24 Jan √	√	suspended 23 Sept; resumed 11 Oct √	suspended 20 May; resumed 11 June √	√
[Philadelphia] Pennsylvania Gazette	√	√	√	√	√	√	suspended 27 Nov √	resumed 5 Feb; sus. 10 Sept (at York 20 Dec) √	(at York to 20 June) √	resumed 5 Jan √
[Philadelphia] Pennsylvania Journal	√	√	√	√	√	√	suspended 27 Nov √	resumed 29 Jan; suspended 17 Sept √	first known after suspension 30 Dec	√
[Philadelphia] Pennsylvania Ledger						from 28 Jan √	suspended 30 Nov √	resumed 10 Oct √	to 23 May √	
[Philadelphia] Pennsylvania Packet		from 28 Oct √	√	√	√	√	suspended 26 Nov; res. 18 Dec √	susp. 9 Sept (at Lancaster from 29 Nov) √	(at Lancaster to 17 June) res. 4 July √	√
[Philadelphia] Pennsylvanische Gazette										only known 3 Feb
[Philadelphia] Penn. Staats-Courier									first & only other known: 11 Feb & 6 May √	
[Philadelphia] Royal Pennsylvania Gazette									from 3 Mar to 26 May √	
Philadelphisches Staatsregister										from 21 July × (suspension?)
[Philadelphia] Story & H's Penn. Mercury						from 7 Apr; last known 22 Dec √				
[Philadelphia] Wochentliche Phila. Staats.		√	√	√	√	√	√	suspended 17 Sept √	resumed 5 Aug √	to 26 May √
RHODE ISLAND										
Newport Gazette								from 16 Jan √	√	last known 6 Oct √

Tables for 1770–1789

RHODE ISLAND continued	1770	1771	1772	1773	1774	1775	1776	1777	1778	1779
Newport Mercury	√	√	√	√	√	√	suspended 2 Dec √			
[Providence] American Journal										from 18 Mar √
Providence Gazette	√	√	√	√	√	√	√	√	√	√
SOUTH CAROLINA										
Charlestown Gazette									(supplement only: 3 Nov)	first known 26 Jan ×
[Charleston] Gazette of the State of S.C.								from 9 Apr √	(suspension in Jan–June) √	√
[Charleston] S.C. & American General Gaz.	√	√	√	×	√	√	suspended 31 May; resumed 2 Aug √	√	√	suspended 30 Apr; resumed 29 May √
[Charleston] South-Carolina Gazette	√	√	suspended 25 Jan; resumed 26 Mar √	√	√	last known 11 Dec √				
[Charleston] S.C. Gaz. & Country Journal	√	√	√	√	√	to 1 Aug √				
VIRGINIA										
[Norfolk] Virginia Gazette					from 9 June √	last known 20 Sept √				
[Norfolk] Virginia Gazette						only known 25 Nov				
[Williamsburg] Virginia Gazette (Hunter)	√	√	√	√	√	√	√	√	last known 4 Dec √	
[Williamsburg] Virginia Gazette (Rind)	√	√	√	√	√	√	last known 3 Feb √			
[Williamsburg] Virginia Gazette (Purdie)						from 3 Feb √	√	√	√	×
[Williamsburg] Virginia Gazette (Dixon)										from 12 Feb √

CONNECTICUT	1780	1781	1782	1783	1784	1785	1786	1787	1788	1789
Fairfield Gazette							first known 26 Oct ×	√	×	last known 23 Sept ×
[Hartford] American Mercury					from 12 July √	√	√	√	√	√
[Hartford] Connecticut Courant	√	√	√	√	√	√	√	√	√	√
[Hartford] Freeman's Chronicle				from 1 Sept √	last known 8 July √					
Litchfield Monitor					from 21 Dec √	√	√	√	√	suspended 8 June; resumed 17 Nov √

Page 13   SYMBOLS: √ complete or extensive coverage exists   × few numbers known (usually less than 25% of those issued)   o no copies extant   Tables for 1770–1789

Chronological Tables of American Newspapers 1690–1820

Table for 1780–1789

CONNECTICUT continued	1780	1781	1782	1783	1784	1785	1786	1787	1788	1789
[Middletown] Middlesex Gazette										✓
New-Haven Chronicle						from 8 Nov	first known 25 Apr ✓	last known 11 Sept ✓		
[New Haven] Connecticut Journal	✓	✓	✓	✓	✓	✓	✓	✓	✓	✓
New-Haven Gazette					from 13 May ✓	✓	to 9 Feb ✓			
New-Haven Gazette & Conn. Magazine							from 16 Feb ✓	✓	✓	last known 18 June ✓
[New London] Connecticut Gazette	✓	✓	✓	✓	✓	✓	✓	✓	✓	✓
Norwich Packet	✓	✓	suspended 26 Sept ✓	resumed 30 Oct ✓	✓	✓	✓	✓	✓	✓
DELAWARE										
[Wilmington] Delaware Courant								first & last known: 5 May & 8 Sept ✓		
[Wilmington] Delaware Gazette						first known 28 June ✗	✗	✗	✗	✓
DISTRICT of COLUMBIA										
[Georgetown] Times & Patowmack Pack.										first known 23 Apr ✗
FLORIDA										
[St. Augustine] East-Florida Gazette				first & last known: 1 Mar & 17 May ✗						
GEORGIA										
Augusta Chronicle										from 11 Apr ✓
[Augusta] Georgia State Gazette							first known 14 Oct ✓	✓	✓	to 4 Apr ✓
[Savannah] Gazette of the State of Georgia				from 30 Jan ✓	✓	✓	✓	✓	to 16 Oct ✓	
[Savannah] Georgia Gazette									from 23 Oct ✓	✓
[Savannah] Royal Georgia Gazette		✓	last known 6 June ✓							
KENTUCKY										
[Lexington] Kentucky Gazette								first known 18 Aug ✓	✓	✓

	1780	1781	1782	1783	1784	1785	1786	1787	1788	1789
MAINE										
[Falmouth] Cumberland Gazette							from 7 Apr to 13 July √	√		
Falmouth Gazette						from 1 Jan √	to 30 Mar √			
[Portland] Cumberland Gazette							from 20 July √	√	√	√
MARYLAND										
[Annapolis] Maryland Gazette	√	√	√	√	√	√	√	√	√	√
[Baltimore] Maryland Gazette				resumed 16 May √	√	√	√	√	√	√
[Baltimore] Maryland Journal	√	√	√	√	√	√	√	√	√	√
[Baltimore] Palladium of Freedom								only known 8 Aug		
[Fredericktown] Bartgis's Md. Zeitung										only known 18 Feb
[Fredericktown] Maryland Chronicle							first known 18 Jan √	√	last known 28 May ×	
[Fredericktown] Maryland Gazette										only known 2 Dec
MASSACHUSETTS										
[Boston] American Herald					from 19 Jan √	√	√	√	to 30 June √	
[Boston] American Journal						first & last known: 15 Mar. & 12 July √				
[Boston] Continental Journal	√	√	√	√	√	√	√	to 21 June √		
[Boston] Courier de Boston										from 23 Apr to 15 Oct √
[Boston] Evening Post	to 11 May √									
Boston Evening-Post		from 20 Oct √	√	√	to 10 Jan √					
[Boston] Exchange Advertiser					from 30 Dec	√	√	to 4 Jan		
Boston Gazette	√	√	√	√	√	√	√	√	√	√
[Boston] Herald of Freedom									from 15 Sept √	√
[Boston] Independent Chronicle	√	√	√	√	√	√	√	√	√	√
[Boston] Independent Ledger	√	√	√	√	√	√	to 16 Oct √			

Page 15   SYMBOLS: √ complete or extensive coverage exists   × few numbers known (usually less than 25% of those issued)   o no copies extant   Table for 1780–1789

Chronological Tables of American Newspapers 1690–1820

MASSACHUSETTS continued	1780	1781	1782	1783	1784	1785	1786	1787	1788	1789
[Boston] Massachusetts Centinel					from 24 Mar ✓	✓	✓	✓	✓	✓
[Boston] Massachusetts Gazette						from 28 Nov ✓	✓	✓	to 11 Nov ✓	
[Charlestown] American Recorder						from 9 Dec ✓	✓	to 25 May ✓		
[Newburyport] Essex Journal					from 9 July ✓	✓	✓	✓	✓	✓
[Northampton] Hampshire Gazette							first known 13 Sept ✓	✓	✓	✓
[Pittsfield] Berkshire Chronicle									from 8 May ✓	✓
Plymouth Journal						from 19 Mar ✓	last known 13 June ✓			
Salem Chronicle		from 2 Jan to 4 Sept ✓								
Salem Gazette							from 30 Mar; last known 3 Aug ✓			
Salem Gazette		from 18 Oct ✓	✓	✓	✓	to 22 Nov ✓				
Salem Mercury							from 14 Oct ✓	✓	✓	to 29 Dec ✓
[Springfield] Hampshire Chronicle								from 6 Mar ✓		
[Springfield] Hampshire Herald					from 27 July ✓	✓	to 26 Sept ✓			
[Springfield] Massachusetts Gazette			from 14 May ✓	✓	to 20 July ✓					
[Stockbridge] Western Star										from 1 Dec ✓
[Worcester] American Herald									from 21 Aug ✓	last known 8 Oct ✓
[Worcester] Massachusetts Herald				from 6 Sept to 27 Sept ✓						
[Worcester] Massachusetts Spy	✓	✓	✓	✓	✓	✓	(as Worcester Magazine after 30 Mar) ✓	(as Worcester Magazine) ✓	(as Worcester Magazine until Apr) ✓	✓
NEW HAMPSHIRE										
Exeter Chronicle					from 10 June; last known 3 Dec ✓					
[Exeter] Freeman's Oracle							from 1 July ✓	✓	✓	last known 12 Nov ✓
[Exeter] New Hampshire Gazetteer								first known 21 Aug ✓		from 18 Aug ✓
[Keene] New-Hampshire Recorder									✓	suspended 27 Nov ✓

	1780	1781	1782	1783	1784	1785	1786	1787	1788	1789
NEW HAMPSHIRE continued										
[Portsmouth] New-Hampshire Gazette	√	√	√	√	√	√	√	√	√	√
[Portsmouth] New-Hampshire Mercury					from 24 Dec √	√	√	√	last known 12 Mar √	
[Portsmouth] New-Hampshire Spy							from 24 Oct √	√	√	√
NEW JERSEY										
[Chatham] New-Jersey Journal	√	√	√	last known 12 Nov √						
[Elizabeth Town] New-Jersey Journal							from 10 May √	√	√	√
[Elizabeth Town] Political Intelligencer						from 20 Apr √	to 3 May √			
[New Brunswick] Brunswick Gazette								first known 3 July √	√	√
New-Brunswick Gazette							only known 5 Oct			
[New Brunswick] Political Intelligencer				from 14 Oct √	√	to 5 Apr √				
Princeton Packet							first known 10 Aug ×	last known 28 June √		
[Springfield] Morning Herald						only known 27 Aug				
[Trenton] Federal Post									first known 5 Aug √	last known 27 Jan ×
Trenton Mercury								from 12 May √	last known 22 Jan ×	
[Trenton] New-Jersey Gazette	√	√	√	suspended 16 July; resumed 9 Dec √	√	√	to 27 Nov √			
NEW YORK										
[Albany] Federal Herald									first & last known: 25 Feb & 7 Apr √	
Albany Gazette						×	√	√		√
Albany Journal									first known 2 Feb √	last known 11 May √
[Albany] New-York Gazetteer			first known 15 July √	√	last known 1 May ×					
Albany Register										first known 6 Apr ×
[Fishkill] New-York Packet	√	√	√	to 28 Aug √						
Goshen Repository										first known 11 Mar √

SYMBOLS: √ complete or extensive coverage exists   × few numbers known (usually less than 25% of those issued)   o no copies extant   Table for 1780–1789

Chronological Tables of American Newspapers 1690–1820

Table for 1780–1789

NEW YORK continued	1780	1781	1782	1783	1784	1785	1786	1787	1788	1789
Hudson Weekly Gazette						from 7 Apr ×	√	√	√	√
[Lansingburgh] Federal Herald									from 28 Apr √	√
[Lansingburgh] Northern Centinel								from 21 May √	last known 15 Jan √	
[New York] American Price-Current							only known 26 June			
[New York] Daily Advertiser						first known 16 Mar √	√	√	√	√
New-York Daily Gazette									from 29 Dec √	√
New-York Evening Post	√		first known 25 Oct ×	last known 21 Mar ×						
New-York Gazette and Weekly Mercury		√	√	last known 10 Nov √						
[New York] Gazette of the United States										from 15 Apr √
New-York Gazetteer				from 3 Dec √	√	√	√	last known 16 Aug √		
[New York] Impartial Gazetteer									from 17 May to 13 Sept √	
[New York] Independent Gazette				from 13 Dec √	to 11 Mar √					
[New York] Independent Journal				from 17 Nov √	√	√	√	√	last known 24 Dec √	
[New York] Independent N.Y. Gazette				from 22 Nov to 6 Dec √						
New-York Journal					from 18 Mar √	√	√	√	√	√
New-York Mercury	×	√	×	last known 15 Aug ×						
New-York Morning Post				first known 25 June ×	√	×	×	√	√	√
New-York Museum									first & last known: 6 June & 15 Aug ×	
New York Packet				from 13 Nov √	√	√	√	√	√	√
New-York Price-Current							only known 14 Aug			
[New York] Rivington's N.Y. Gazette				from 22 Nov to 31 Dec √						
[New York] Royal American Gazette	√	×	×	last known 7 Aug ×						
[New York] Royal Gazette	√	√	√	to 19 Nov √						

	1780	1781	1782	1783	1784	1785	1786	1787	1788	1789
NEW YORK continued										
[New York] Town and Country Journal				from 11 Sept; last known 11 Dec √						
New-York Weekly Museum									from 20 Sept √	√
[Poughkeepsie] Country Journal						first known 15 Sept √	√	√	√	to 7 July √
Poughkeepsie Journal										from 14 July √
[Poughkeepsie] New-York Journal	suspended 6 Nov √	resumed 30 July √	to 6 Jan √							
NORTH CAROLINA										
Edenton Intelligencer								only known 19 Dec	first & only other known: 9 Apr & 4 June	
[Edenton] North-Carolina Gazette										
[Edenton] State Gazette of North-Carolina									first known 8 Sept √	√
Fayetteville Gazette										from 24 Aug; last known 12 Oct √
[Hillsborough] North Carolina Gazette						first known 6 Oct	only other known 16 Feb			
[New Bern] North Carolina Gazette					first & only other known: 29 July & 2 Sept.			first known 11 July ×		
[New Bern] North-Carolina Gazette								first known 9 Aug ×	o	o
[New Bern] State Gazette of N.C.									last known 27 Mar ×	
Wilmington Centinel									only known 18 June	
PENNSYLVANIA										
Carlisle Gazette						from 10 Aug √	√	√	√	√
Germantauner Zeitung						first known 22 Feb √	√	√	√	√
Harrisburgh Journal										only known 9 Sept
[Lancaster] Neue Unpartheyische L. Zeit.								from 8 Aug √	√	√
[Philadelphia] Allied Mercury		from 17 Oct; only other known 30 Nov								
[Philadelphia] American Herald					first & last known: 28 June & 5 July √					
[Philadelphia] Complete C. H. Companion						first known 19 Mar √	√	√	×	√

Page 19   SYMBOLS: √ complete or extensive coverage exists   × few numbers known (usually less than 25 % of those issued)   o no copies extant   Table for 1780–1789

Chronological Tables of American Newspapers 1690–1820

Table for 1780–1789

PENNSYLVANIA continued	1780	1781	1782	1783	1784	1785	1786	1787	1788	1789
[Philadelphia] Courier de l'Amérique					from 27 July to 26 Oct ✓					
[Philadelphia] Evening Chronicle								first & last known: 13 Feb & 7 Nov ✓		
[Philadelphia] Federal Gazette									from 8 Mar to 24 Apr ✓	
[Philadelphia] Federal Gazette									from 1 Oct ✓	✓
[Philadelphia] Freeman's Journal		from 25 Apr ✓	✓	✓	✓	✓	✓	✓	✓	✓
[Philadelphia] Gemeinnützige Phila. Cor.		first known 18 July ✓	✓	✓	✓	✓	✓	✓	✓	✓
[Philadelphia] Independent Gazetteer			from 13 Apr ✓	✓	✓	✓	✓	✓	✓	✓
[Philadelphia] Penn. Evening Herald					last known 26 Oct ✗	from 25 Jan ✓	✓	✓	last known 14 Feb ✓	
[Philadelphia] Pennsylvania Evening Post	✓	✓	✓	✓	✓	✓	✓	✓	✓	✓
[Philadelphia] Pennsylvania Gazette	✓	✓	✓	✓	✓	✓	✓	✓	✓	✓
[Philadelphia] Pennsylvania Journal	✓	✓	✓	✓	✓	✓	✓	✓	✓	✓
[Philadelphia] Pennsylvania Mercury					from 20 Aug ✓	✓	✓	✓	✓	✓
[Philadelphia] Pennsylvania Packet	✓	✓	✓	✓	✓	✓	✓	✓	✓	✓
Philadelphia Price Current	(suspension?) last known 24 May ✗			first known 26 Aug ✗	✗	last known 28 Nov ✗				
Philadelphisches Staatsregister										
Pittsburgh Gazette							first known 12 Aug ✓	✓	✓	✓
[Reading] Neue Unpartheyische R. Zeit.										from 18 Feb ✓
[York] Pennsylvania Chronicle								first known 7 Nov ✗	last known 2 Apr ✗	
[York] Pennsylvania Herald										from 7 Jan ✓
RHODE ISLAND										
[Newport] Gazette Françoise	from 17 Nov ✓	last known 2 Jan (supplement)								
Newport Herald								from 1 Mar ✓	✓	✓
Newport Mercury	resumed 5 Jan ✓	✓	✓	✓	✓	✓	✓	suspended 8 Nov; res. 22 Dec ✓	✓	✓

RHODE ISLAND continued	1780	1781	1782	1783	1784	1785	1786	1787	1788	1789
[Providence] American Journal	✓	to 29 Aug ✓								
Providence Gazette	✓	✓	✓	✓	✓	✓	✓	✓	✓	✓
[Providence] United States Chronicle					from 1 Jan ✓	✓	✓	✓	✓	✓
SOUTH CAROLINA										
[Charleston] Chronicle of Liberty				only known 25 Mar						
[Charleston] City Gazette								from 6 Nov ✓	✓	✓
[Charleston] Columbian Herald					from 23 Nov ✓	✓	✓	✓	✓	✗
Charleston Evening Gazette						from 11 July ✓	last known 18 Oct ✓			
Charlestown Gazette	last known 18 Jan ✓									
[Charleston] Gazette of the State of S.C.	suspended 9 Feb ✗			resumed 16 July ✓	✓	to 24 Mar ✓				
Charleston Morning Post							from 18 Jan ✓	to 5 Nov ✓		
[Charleston] Royal Gazette		from 3 Mar ✓	(suspension) last known 28 Sept ✓							
[Charleston] Royal South-Carolina Gazette	first known 8 June ✗	✗	last known 12 Sept ✗							
[Charleston] S.C. & American General Gaz.	(suspension?) ✓	to 28 Feb ✓								
[Charleston] S.C. Gaz. and General Adv.				from 15 Mar ✓	✓	last known 26 July ✓				
[Charleston] South-Carolina Weekly Adv.				from 19 Feb; last known 23 Apr ✓						
[Charleston] S.C. Weekly Chronicle								only known 9 Oct		
[Charleston] South-Carolina Weekly Gaz.				from 15 Feb ✓	✓	✓	to 14 Jan ✓			
[Charleston] State Gaz. of South-Carolina						from 28 Mar ✓	✓	✓	✓	✗
[Parker's Ferry] South-Carolina Gazette			only known 15 May							
VERMONT										
[Bennington] Vermont Gazette				from 5 June ✓	✓	✓	✓	✓	✓	✓
[Westminster] Vermont Gazette		first & only other known: 2 Apr & 9 July								

Page 21   SYMBOLS: √ complete or extensive coverage exists   × few numbers known (usually less than 25 % of those issued)   o no copies extant   Table for 1780–1789

Chronological Tables of American Newspapers 1690–1820

VERMONT continued	1780	1781	1782	1783	1784	1785	1786	1787	1788	1789
[Windsor] Vermont Journal				from 7 Aug √	√	√	√	√	√	√
VIRGINIA										
[Alexandria] Virginia Gazette										first known 3 Sept ×
[Alexandria] Virginia Journal					from 5 Feb √	√	√	√	×	last known 21 May ×
[Fredericksburg] Virginia Herald								first known 6 Sept ×	√	√
Norfolk and Portsmouth Chronicle										first known 26 Sept ×
Norfolk and Portsmouth Gazette										first & last known: 23 Sept & 8 Oct √
Norfolk and Portsmouth Journal							first known 8 Nov (mutilated) ×	×	√	last known 6 May √
[Petersburg] Virginia Gazette							first known 14 Sept √	×	×	o
[Richmond] Virginia Gazette	from 9 May √	(suspension) last known 19 May √								
[Richmond] Va. Gazette & Ind. Chronicle				first known 15 Nov √	×	×	√	×	×	last known 4 July (supplement) ×
[Richmond] Va. Gazette and Public Adv.										first known 3 Oct ×
[Richmond] Va. Gazette and Weekly Adv.			first known 5 Jan √	√	√	√	×	√	√	√
[Richmond] Va. Gazette or Amer. Adv.		from 22 Dec √	√	√	√	√	last known 20 Dec √			
[Richmond] Va. Independent Chronicle							from 26 July √	√	√	√
[Williamsburg] Virginia Gazette (Purdie)	last known 9 Dec ×									
[Williamsburg] Virginia Gazette (Dixon)	to 8 Apr √									
[Winchester] Virginia Centinel										
[Winchester] Virginia Gazette										

	1790	1791	1792	1793	1794	1795	1796	1797	1798	1799
[Winchester] Virginia Centinel								from 11 July √		
[Winchester] Virginia Gazette									first known 9 Apr √	
CONNECTICUT										
[Danbury] Farmers Chronicle				first known 5 Aug √	×	√	last known 19 Sept √			
[Danbury] Farmer's Journal	from 18 Mar √	√	√	last known 27 May √						
				first & last known: 1 July						

CONNECTICUT continued	1790	1791	1792	1793	1794	1795	1796	1797	1798	1799
[Danbury] Republican Journal							from 3 Oct √	√	√	×
[Hartford] American Mercury	√	√	√	√	√	√	√	√	√	√
[Hartford] Connecticut Courant	√	√	√	√	√	√	√	√	√	√
Hartford Gazette					from 13 Jan √	to 19 Mar √				
[Hartford] New Star							only known 2 Feb			
Litchfield Monitor	√	√	√	√	√	√	√	√	√	√
[Middletown] Middlesex Gazette	√	√	suspended 28 Jan; resumed 25 Feb √	√	√	√	√	√	√	√
[New Haven] Connecticut Journal	√	√	√	√	√	√	√	√	√	√
[New Haven] Federal Gazetteer							first known 9 Apr √	last known 5 Apr ×		
New-Haven Gazette		from 5 Jan to 29 June √								
New-London Advertiser						first & last known: 16 Mar. & 13 Apr √				
[New London] Bee								from 14 June √	suspended 5 Sept; resumed 14 Nov √	√
[New London] Connecticut Gazette	√	√	√	√	√	√	√	√	√	√
[New London] Weekly Oracle						from 8 Apr √	from 22 Oct √	√	√	√
[Newfield] American Telegraphe							√	√	×	×
[Newfield] Humming Bird									from 14 Apr; only other known 9 June	
[Norwich] Courier							from 30 Nov √	√	√	√
Norwich Packet	√	√	√	√	√	√	√	√	√	√
[Norwich] Weekly Register		from 29 Nov √	√	√	√	to 19 Aug √				
[Stonington] Impartial Journal										from 8 Oct √
[Stonington] Journal of the Times									from 10 Oct √	last known 17 Sept √
[Suffield] Impartial Herald								from 14 June √	√	last known 11 June √
Windham Herald		from 12 Mar √	√	√	√	√	√	√	√	√

SYMBOLS: √ complete or extensive coverage exists × few numbers known (usually less than 25% of those issued) o no copies extant

Table for 1790–1799

Chronological Tables of American Newspapers 1690–1820

Table for 1790–1799

	1790	1791	1792	1793	1794	1795	1796	1797	1798	1799
DELAWARE										
[Dover] Friend of the People										only known 28 Sept
[Wilmington] Del. & Eastern-Shore Adv.					from 14 May √	√	√	√	√	last known 26 Dec
[Wilmington] Delaware Gazette	√	√	√	√	√	√	√	√	(suspension in Sept–Oct) ×	to 7 Sept √
Wilmington Mercury									first & last known: 16 Sept & 25 Oct √	
[Wilmington] Mirror of the Times										from 20 Nov √
DISTRICT of COLUMBIA										
[Georgetown] Centinel & Country Gazette								first known 30 June ×	×	o
[Georgetown] Centinel of Liberty							first known 27 May √	×	×	√
[Georgetown] Columbian Chronicle				from 3 Dec ×	×	√	last known 10 May √			
[Georgetown] Times & Patowmack Pack.	√	last known 6 July ×								
Georgetown Weekly Ledger	first known 1 May ×	√	×	last known 5 Oct ×						
Washington Advertiser							from 9 Mar; last known 11 May			
Washington Gazette							from 15 June √	suspended 26 July; resumed 16 Sept √	last known 24 Mar √	
[Washington] Impartial Observer						first & last known: 12 June & 1 Oct √				
GEORGIA										
Augusta Chronicle	√	√	√	√	√	√	√	√	√	√
Augusta Herald										from 17 July √
[Augusta] Southern Centinel				from 6 June √	√	√	√	√	√	last known 7 Nov √
Louisville Gazette										from 22 Jan √
[Louisville] State Gazette										first & last known: 20 Aug & 24 Dec √
[Savannah] Columbian Museum							from 4 Mar √	√	√	√
[Savannah] Georgia Gazette	√	√	√	√	√	√	suspended 24 Nov √	resumed 2 Sept √	√	√
[Savannah] Georgia Journal				from 4 Dec √	last known 19 Feb √					

	1790	1791	1792	1793	1794	1795	1796	1797	1798	1799
KENTUCKY										
[Frankfort] Guardian of Freedom									from 8 May √	√
[Frankfort] Kentucky Journal						only known 5 Dec				
[Frankfort] Palladium									from 9 Aug √	√
[Lexington] Kentucky Gazette	√	√	√	√	√	√	√	√	√	√
[Lexington] Stewart's Kentucky Herald						first known 30 June √	×	×	×	×
[Paris] Rights of Man								first known 30 Aug √	last known 10 Jan ×	
[Washington] Mirror								first known 30 Sept √	√	last known 18 Sept √
LOUISIANA										
[New Orleans] Moniteur de la Louisiane					first known 25 Aug ×	o	o	o	o	o
MAINE										
[Augusta] Kennebeck Intelligencer						from 21 Nov √	√	√	√	√
Castine Journal										from 2 Jan √
[Fryeburg] Russel's Echo									from 22 Feb √	to 11 Jan ×
[Hallowell] Eastern Star						first & last known: 20 Jan & 21 July √				
[Hallowell] Tocsin						from 4 Aug ×	√	last known 25 Aug √		
[Portland] Cumberland Gazette	√	to 26 Dec √								
[Portland] Eastern Herald			from 2 Jan √	√	√	√	√	√	√	√
[Portland] Gazette									from 16 Apr √	√
[Portland] Gazette of Maine	from 8 Oct √	√	√	√	√	√	to 29 Aug √			
[Portland] Oriental Trumpet							from 15 Dec √	√	√	√
Wiscasset Argus								first known 30 Dec	last known 13 Jan √	
Wiscasset Telegraph							first known 10 Dec √	√	×	last known 9 Mar ×

Page 25   SYMBOLS: √ complete or extensive coverage exists   × few numbers known (usually less than 25% of those issued)   o no copies extant   Table for 1790–1799

Chronological Tables of American Newspapers 1690–1820

Table for 1790–1799

MARYLAND	1790	1791	1792	1793	1794	1795	1796	1797	1798	1799
[Annapolis] Maryland Gazette	√	√	√	√	√	√	√	√	√	√
[Baltimore] American										from 14 May √
[Baltimore] City Gazette								first & last known: 11 Feb. & 12 Apr √		
Baltimore Daily Intelligencer				from 28 Oct √	to 29 Oct √					
Baltimore Daily Repository		from 24 Oct √	√	last known 19 Oct √						
[Baltimore] Eagle of Freedom							first & last known: 15 July. & 27 July √			
[Baltimore] Edwards's Balt. Daily Adv.				first known 21 Oct √	last known 18 Dec ×					
Baltimore Evening Post			from 13 July √	last known 30 Sept ×						
[Baltimore] Federal Gazette							from 1 Jan √	√	√	√
[Baltimore] Federal Intelligencer					from 30 Oct √	to 30 Dec √				
[Baltimore] Fell's-Point Telegraphe						first & last known: 6 Mar & 1 June ×				
Baltimore Intelligencer									from 7 Mar √	last known 7 Feb √
[Baltimore] Maryland Gazette	√	√	to 6 Jan √							
[Baltimore] Maryland Journal	√	√	√	√	√	√				
[Baltimore] Neue Unpartheyische B. Bote							only known 4 May √			
[Baltimore] Sunday Monitor							only known 18 Dec			
Baltimore Telegraphe						from 23 Mar √	√	√	√	√
[Baltimore] Weekly Museum								from 8 Jan; last known 28 May √		
[Chestertown] Apollo				first & last known: 26 Mar. & 31 Dec √						
[Easton] Maryland Herald	from 11 May √	√	√	√	√	√	√	√	√	√
[Elizabethtown] Maryland Herald								from 2 Mar √	√	√
[Elizabethtown] Washington Spy	first known 26 Aug √	√	√	√	√	√	√	last known 1 Feb √		
[Fredericktown] Bartgis's Federal Gazette						first known 26 Feb ×	√	√	√	√

MARYLAND continued	1790	1791	1792	1793	1794	1795	1796	1797	1798	1799
[Fredericktown] Bartgis's Md. Gazette			from 22 May √	√	last known 23 Jan √					
[Fredericktown] General Staats-Bothe				from 5 Jan to 21 Dec √						
[Fredericktown] Maryland Gazette	first known 11 Dec √	last known 4 Oct ×								
[Fredericktown] Rights of Man					first known 5 Feb ×	√	√	√	×	○
[Hagerstown] Westliche Correspondenz							first known 28 Sept ×	○	×	○
MASSACHUSETTS										
[Boston] American Apollo			from 6 Jan √	√	to 25 Dec √					
[Boston] Argus		from 22 July √	√	last known 28 June √						
[Boston] Columbian Centinel	from 16 June √	√	√	√	√	√	√	√	√	√
[Boston] Constitutional Telegraph										from 2 Oct √
[Boston] Courier						from 1 July √	to 5 Mar √			
[Boston] Federal Gazette									from 1 Jan to 26 Mar √	
[Boston] Federal Orrery					from 20 Oct √	√	to 8 Dec √			
Boston Gazette	√	√	√	√	√	√	√	√	to 17 Sept √	
[Boston] Herald of Freedom	√	to 19 July √								
[Boston] Independent Chronicle	√	√	√	√	√	√	√	√	√	√
[Boston] Massachusetts Centinel	to 12 June √									
[Boston] Massachusetts Mercury				from 1 Jan √	√	√	√	√	√	√
[Boston] Polar Star							from 6 Oct √	last known 2 Feb √		
Boston Price–Current						from 7 Sept √	√	√	to 4 June √	
[Boston] Russell's Gazette									from 7 June √	√
[Boston] Saturday Evening Herald	first & last known: 24 July & 13 Dec √									
[Boston] Times					from 4 Oct; last known 8 Nov √					

Page 27   SYMBOLS: √ complete or extensive coverage exists   × few numbers known (usually less than 25% of those issued)   ○ no copies extant   Table for 1790–1799

Chronological Tables of American Newspapers 1690–1820

Table for 1790–1799

MASSACHUSETTS continued	1790	1791	1792	1793	1794	1795	1796	1797	1798	1799
[Brookfield] Moral & Political Telegraphe							to 17 Aug √			
[Brookfield] Political Repository									from 14 Aug √	√
[Brookfield] Worcester Intelligencer					from 7 Oct √	to 28 Apr √				
[Conway] Farmer's Register									first & last known: 7 Apr & 27 Oct √	
[Dedham] Columbian Minerva										from 3 Jan √
[Dedham] Minerva							from 11 Oct √	√	to 27 Dec √	
Greenfield Gazette			from 2 Aug √	√	√	√	√	√	√	√
[Greenfield] Impartial Intelligencer			from 1 Feb to 26 July √							
Haverhill Federal Gazette									from 26 Oct √	to 27 Nov √
[Haverhill] Guardian of Freedom				from 16 Sept √	√	last known 5 Nov √				
[Haverhill] Impartial Herald									from 27 July to 19 Oct √	
[Leominster] Political Focus									first known 12 July √	last known 5 Dec √
[Leominster] Rural Repository						from 22 Oct √	√	to 13 Apr √		
[New Bedford] Columbian Courier									from 8 Dec √	√
[New Bedford] Medley			from 27 Nov √	√	√	√	√	√	√	to 18 Oct √
[Newburyport] Essex Journal	√	√	√	√	to 2 Apr √					
Newburyport Herald								from 31 Oct √	√	√
[Newburyport] Impartial Herald				from 18 May √	√	√	√	to 27 Oct √		
[Newburyport] Morning Star					from 8 Apr to 3 Dec √					
[Newburyport] Political Gazette						from 30 Apr √	√	to 27 Oct √		
[Northampton] Hampshire Gazette	√	√	√	√	√	√	√	√	√	√
[Northampton] Patriotic Gazette										from 12 Apr √
[Pittsfield] Berkshire Chronicle	last known 30 Sept √									

MASSACHUSETTS continued	1790	1791	1792	1793	1794	1795	1796	1797	1798	1799
[Pittsfield] Berkshire Gazette									from 18 Jan ✓	✓
Salem Gazette	from 5 Jan ✓	✓	✓	✓	✓	✓	✓	✓	✓	✓
[Springfield] Federal Spy			from 19 Dec ✓	✓	✓	✓	✓	✓	×	✓
[Springfield] Hampshire Chronicle	✓	✓	✓	✓	✓	✓	to 6 Sept ✓			
[Stockbridge] Western Star	✓	✓	✓	✓	✓	✓	✓	✓	✓	✓
[West Springfield] American Intelligencer						first known 25 Aug ✓	✓	last known 28 Nov ✓		
[Worcester] Massachusetts Spy	✓	✓	✓	✓	✓	✓	✓	✓	✓	✓
NEW HAMPSHIRE										
Amherst Journal						from 16 Jan ✓	to 9 Jan ✓			
[Amherst] Village Messenger							from 9 Jan ✓	✓	✓	✓
[Concord] Courier of New Hampshire					from 13 Feb ✓	✓	✓	✓	✓	✓
Concord Herald	from 6 Jan ✓	✓	✓	✓	to 6 Feb ✓					
[Concord] Mirrour			from 6 Sept (prospectus number) ✓	✓	✓	✓	suspended 15 Nov ✓	resumed 10 Oct ✓	✓	last known 2 Sept ✓
[Concord] New Star								from 11 Apr to 3 Oct ✓		
[Concord] Republican Gazetteer							from 22 Nov ✓	to 4 Apr ✓		
[Dover] Phoenix			first known 8 Feb ✓	✓	×	last known 22 Aug ✓				
[Dover] Political and Sentimental Repos.	first known 29 July ✓	✓	last known 4 Jan ✓							
[Dover] Sun						first known 12 Sept ✓	✓	✓	✓	✓
[Exeter] Herald of Liberty				from 20 Feb ✓	✓	✓	last known 12 July ✓			
[Exeter] Lamson's Weekly Visitor						from 5 May; last known 26 Dec ✓				
[Exeter] New Hampshire Gazetteer		✓	✓	to 13 Feb ✓						
[Exeter] New-Hampshire Spy	✓	✓					from 24 Sept ✓	to 18 Mar ✓		
[Exeter] Political Banquet										first & last known; 8 Oct & 31 Dec ×

Page 29   SYMBOLS: ✓ complete or extensive coverage   × few numbers known (usually less than 25 % of those issued)   o no copies extant   Table for 1790–1799

Chronological Tables of American Newspapers 1690–1820

Table for 1790–1799

NEW HAMPSHIRE continued	1790	1791	1792	1793	1794	1795	1796	1797	1798	1799
[Exeter] Ranlet's Federal Miscellany									first known 12 Dec √	last known 24 Sept ✗
Gilmanton Rural Museum										first known 11 Nov ✗
[Hanover] Dartmouth Gazette										from 27 Aug √
[Hanover] Eagle				from 22 July √	√	√	√	√	√	last known 1 June √
[Haverhill] Grafton Minerva							first known 24 Mar √	last known 23 Jan √		
[Keene] Cheshire Advertiser			first & last known: 19 Jan & 6 Dec ✗							
[Keene] Columbian Informer				first known 18 Apr √	√	last known 30 June √				
[Keene] New-Hampshire Recorder	resumed 18 Mar √	last known 24 Feb √								
[Keene] New Hampshire Sentinel										from 23 Mar √
[Keene] Rising Sun						from 11 Aug √	√	√	last known 23 June √	
[Portsmouth] Federal Observer									from 22 Nov √	√
[Portsmouth] New-Hampshire Gazette	√	√	√	√	√	√	√	√	√	√
[Portsmouth] New-Hampshire Spy	√	√	√	to 2 Mar √						
[Portsmouth] Oracle of the Day				from 4 June √	√	√	√	√	√	to 28 Dec √
[Portsmouth] Republican Ledger										first known 19 Sept √
[Walpole] Farmer's Weekly Museum								from 4 Apr √	√	√
[Walpole] New Hampshire Journal				from 11 Apr √	√	√	√	to 28 Mar √		
NEW JERSEY										
[Bridgeton] Argus						first known 5 Nov √	last known 10 Nov √			
Burlington Advertiser	from 13 Apr √	to 13 Dec √								
[Elizabeth Town] New-Jersey Journal	√	√	√	√	√	√	√	√	√	√
[Morristown] Genius of Liberty									from 24 May √	√
[Morristown] Morris County Gazette								from 24 May √	to 15 May √	

NEW JERSEY continued	1790	1791	1792	1793	1794	1795	1796	1797	1798	1799
[Mount Pleasant] Jersey Chronicle						from 2 May √	to 30 Apr √			
[New Brunswick] Arnett's Bruns. Adv.				only known 12 Nov						
[New Brunswick] Arnett's N.J. Federalist					first known 3 July ×	last known 26 Feb ×				
[New Brunswick] Brunswick Gazette	√	√	to 30 Oct √							
[New Brunswick] Genius of Liberty						first known 22 June √	last known 22 Feb ×			
[New Brunswick] Guardian			from 7 Nov √	√	√	√	√	√	√	√
[New Brunswick] New-Jersey Federalist						from 12 Mar; last known 7 May √				
[Newark] Centinel of Freedom							from 5 Oct √	√	√	√
Newark Gazette		from 19 May √	√	√	√	√	√	to 1 Nov √		
[Newark] Woods's Newark Gazette								from 8 Nov √	√	√
[Newton] Farmers Journal							first known 5 Feb ×	×	last known 17 Oct ×	
[Salem] Observer										only known 4 May
[Trenton] Federalist									from 9 July √	√
[Trenton] New-Jersey State Gazette			from 12 Sept √	√	√	√	to 5 July √			
[Trenton] New-Jersey State Gazette										from 5 Mar √
[Trenton] State Gazette							from 12 July √	√	√	to 26 Feb √
NEW YORK										
Albany Centinel								from 4 July √	√	√
Albany Chronicle							from 12 Sept; last kn. before susp. 17 Oct √	resumed 2 Jan √	last known 9 Apr √	
Albany Gazette	√	√	√	√	√	√	√	√	√	√
Albany Register	√	√	√	√	√	√	√	√	√	√
[Ballston Spa] Saratoga Register									first & only other known: 5 Sept & 21 Nov.	
Bath Gazette								first known 5 Jan √	last known 12 Apr √	

SYMBOLS: √ complete or extensive coverage exists   × few numbers known (usually less than 25% of those issued)   o no copies extant   Table for 1790–1799

Chronological Tables of American Newspapers 1690–1820

Table for 1790–1799

NEW YORK continued	1790	1791	1792	1793	1794	1795	1796	1797	1798	1799
[Brooklyn] Long Island Courier										first known 11 July √
[Canaan] Columbian Mercury					only known 1 Oct					
[Canandaigua] Ontario Gazette										first known 16 July √
Catskill Packet			from 6 Aug √	√	√	√	√	√	suspended 29 Dec √	resumed 9 Mar; to 29 Aug √
[Cooperstown] Otsego Herald						from 3 Apr √	√	√	√	√
[Geneva] Ontario Gazette							from 24 Nov ×	×	×	last known 8 Jan ×
Goshen Repository	×	√	√	√	√	√	√	√	√	to 31 Dec √
Hudson Gazette			first known 15 Mar ×	×	×	√	√	√	√	√
Hudson Weekly Gazette	√	last known 10 Nov ×								
Johnstown Gazette						from 15 July ×	×	×	last known 28 Nov ×	
[Kingston] Farmer's Register			first known 6 Oct √	last known 14 Sept √						
[Kingston] Rising Sun				from 28 Sept √	√	√	×	√	to 28 Apr √	
[Kingston] Ulster County Gazette									first known 12 May ×	×
[Lansingburgh] American Spy		from 8 Apr √	√	√	√	√	√	(suspension)	last known 27 Feb √	
[Lansingburgh] Farmer's Oracle							from 1 Nov; last known 13 Dec √			
[Lansingburgh] Federal Herald	to 7 June √									
Lansingburgh Gazette	√								from 18 Sept √	√
[Lansingburgh] Northern Budget								from 20 June √	to 8 May √	
Lansingburgh Recorder					from 9 Dec √	last known 12 May ×				
[Lansingburgh] Tiffany's Recorder				first known 11 June ×	last known 23 Sept ×					
Mount Pleasant Courier										only known 19 June
New-Windsor Gazette									first & only other known: 16 Jan & 28 Aug.	
[New York] American Minerva				from 9 Dec √	√	√	to 30 Apr √			

NEW YORK continued	1790	1791	1792	1793	1794	1795	1796	1797	1798	1799
[New York] Argus						from 11 May √	√	√	suspended 15 Sept; resumed 5 Nov √	√
[New York] Columbian Gazette										from 6 Apr to 22 June √
[New York] Columbian Gazetteer				from 22 Aug √	to 13 Nov √					
[New York] Commercial Advertiser								from 2 Oct √	√	√
[New York] Daily Advertiser	√	√	√	√	√	√	√	√	√	√
New-York Daily Gazette	√	√	√	√	√	last known 25 Apr ×				
[New York] Diary			from 15 Feb √	√	√	√	√	√	last known 13 Sept √	
[New York] Evening Mercury				from 1 Jan; only other known 3 Jan						
New-York Evening Post					from 17 Nov √	to 25 May √				
New-York Gazette						first known 29 Jan √	√	√	√	√
[New York] Gazette Francaise						from 6 July √	√	√	√	last known 4 Oct √
[New York] Gazette of the United States	to 13 Oct √									
[New York] Greenleaf's New York Journal					from 1 Jan √	√	√	√	suspended 16 Sept; resumed 7 Nov √	√
[New York] Herald					from 4 June √	√	√	to 30 Sept √		
New-York Journal	√	√	√	to 28 Dec √						
[New York] Journal des Révolutions				only known 16 Sept (plus suppl. to #1)						
[New York] Mercantile Advertiser									first known 13 Nov √	√
[New York] Minerva							from 2 May √	to 30 Sept √		
New-York Morning Post	√	√	last known 12 June √							
[New York] Mott & Hurtin's Chronicle						from 1 Jan to 16 Apr √				
New York Packet	√	√	to 26 Jan √							
New-York Price-Current								first known 2 Jan √	√	√
[New York] Register of the Times							from 3 June √	√	last known 27 June ×	

Page 33   SYMBOLS: √ complete or extensive coverage exists   × few numbers known (usually less than 25% of those issued)   o no copies extant   Table for 1790–1799

Chronological Tables of American Newspapers 1690–1820

Table for 1790–1799

NEW YORK continued	1790	1791	1792	1793	1794	1795	1796	1797	1798	1799
[New York] Spectator								from 4 Oct ·	√	√
[New York] Tablet								first known 13 Dec √	last known 27 June ×	
[New York] Time Piece								from 13 Mar √	last known 30 Aug √	
New-York Weekly Chronicle						first & last known: 30 Apr. & 1 Oct √				
New-York Weekly Museum	√	√	√	√	√	√	√	√	suspended 8 Sept; resumed 10 Nov √	suspended 7 Sept; resumed 2 Nov √
[New York] Youth's News Paper								from 30 Sept to 4 Nov √		
[Newburgh] Mirror									first known 15 Oct √	last known 3 Sept √
[Newburgh] Orange County Gazette										only known 31 Dec
Newburgh Packet						first known 3 Feb ×	√	last known 10 Jan (plus 5 June suppl.) √		
[Poughkeepsie] American Farmer									from 8 June √	√
Poughkeepsie Journal	√	√	√	√	√	√	√	√	√	√
[Poughkeepsie] Republican Journal						first known 21 Oct √	last known 6 July √			
[Rome] Columbian Patriotic Gazette										first known 26 Sept ×
[Sag Harbor] Frothingham's L. I. Herald		from 10 May √	×	×	×	×	×	√	last known 17 Dec √	
[Salem] Northern Centinel									from 1 Jan √	
[Salem] Times					from 18 June; only other known 26 June					
[Salem] Washington Patrol						from 27 May; last known 18 Nov √				
Schenectady Gazette										first known 31 Dec
[Schenectady] Mohawk Mercury						first known 9 Feb √	√	√	last known 13 Mar √	
[Scipio] Levana Gazette									first & only other known: 21 Nov & 5 Dec.	
[Troy] Farmer's Oracle								first known 28 Feb √	last known 17 Apr √	
[Troy] Northern Budget									from 15 May √	√
[Troy] Recorder						first & last known: 26 May. & 8 Dec √				

	1790	1791	1792	1793	1794	1795	1796	1797	1798	1799
NEW YORK continued										
[Upton] Columbian Courier					first & only other known: 9 & 16 Sept					
[Utica] Whitestown Gazette									first known 3 Sept ×	√
Whitestown Gazette				from 11 July; last kn. before susp. 22 Aug ×			first known after suspension 5 July √		last known 12 June √	
[Whitestown] Western Centinel					first known 26 Mar ×	×	√	√	last known 2 Nov ×	
NORTH CAROLINA										
[Edenton] Herald of Freedom	first known 1 Feb √									first & only other known: 27 Mar & 1 May
[Edenton] State Gazette of North-Carolina	√	√	×	×	√	√	√	√	×	last known 20 Feb √
Fayetteville Gazette			from 7 Aug √	last known 19 Nov ×						
[Fayetteville] North-Carolina Centinel						first & last known: 25 July & 29 Aug √				
[Fayetteville] North-Carolina Chronicle	first known 1 Feb √	to 7 Mar √								
[Fayetteville] North-Carolina Minerva							first known 31 Mar √	√	√	last known 23 Mar √
[Halifax] North-Carolina Journal			first known 26 July √	√	√	√	√	√	√	√
Newbern Gazette									first known 25 Aug √	×
[New Bern] North-Carolina Gazette	×	×	o	√	√	√	√	×	last known 24 Feb ×	
[Raleigh] North-Carolina Minerva									first known 28 May √	
Raleigh Register										from 22 Oct
[Salisbury] North-Carolina Mercury									first known 27 June ×	
Wilmington Chronicle						from 3 July ×	last known 4 Aug ×			
Wilmington Gazette										first known 7 Mar √
[Wilmington] Hall's Wilmington Gazette								first known 9 Feb √	last known 29 Nov ×	
OHIO										
[Cincinnati] Centinel of N. W. Territory				from 9 Nov √	√	√	last known 4 June √			
[Cincinnati] Freeman's Journal							first known 9 July √	×	×	last known 1 Oct ×

Page 35   SYMBOLS: √ complete or extensive coverage exists   × few numbers known (usually less than 25% of those issued)   o no copies extant   Table for 1790–1799

Chronological Tables of American Newspapers 1690–1820

Table for 1790–1799

OHIO continued	1790	1791	1792	1793	1794	1795	1796	1797	1798	1799
[Cincinnati] Western Spy										from 28 May √
PENNSYLVANIA										
Carlisle Gazette	√	√	√	√	√	√	√	√	√	√
[Carlisle] Telegraphe						from 10 Feb √	last known 3 May √			
[Chambersburg] Farmers' Register									from 18 Apr √	to 10 Apr √
[Chambersburg] Franklin Repository							first known 5 May √	√	o	×
Chambersburg Gazette				first known 17 Oct √	×	×	to 7 Apr √			
[Chestnut Hill] Chestnut. Wochenschrift	(prospectus issue 8 Oct) from 15 Dec √	√	√	last known 20 Aug √						
[Easton] American Eagle										from 10 May √
[Easton] Neuer Unpartheyischer E. Bothe					first known 24 Sept √	×	o	o	o	o
Germantauner Zeitung	√	√	√	last known 24 Dec √						
[Greensburg] Farmers Register										from 24 May √
Harrisburg Monitor		only known 1 Feb								
Harrisburger Morgenröthe Zeitung										from 12 Mar √
[Harrisburgh] Oracle of Dauphin			from 20 Oct √	√	√	√	√	√	√	√
Huntingdon Courier								only known 8 Aug		
Lancaster Correspondent										from 25 May √
[Lancaster] Deutsche Porcupein									from 3 Jan √	to 25 Dec √
[Lancaster] Hive								from 31 May √	to 23 May √	
[Lancaster] Intelligencer										from 31 July √
Lancaster Journal					first known 13 Aug ×	√	√	√	√	√
[Lancaster] Neue Unpartheyische L. Zeit.	√	√	√	√	×	o	×	last known 1 Nov ×		
[Lewistown] Monitor									first known 22 Dec	only other known 9 Feb

PENNSYLVANIA continued	1790	1791	1792	1793	1794	1795	1796	1797	1798	1799
[Mifflintown] Mifflin & Huntingdon Gaz.										(preliminary issue 1 June) from 15 June √
Norristown Gazette										
[Northumberland] Sunbury & N. Gazette				first known 9 Oct ×	√	×	only known 20 July ×	o	×	×
[Philadelphia] American Star					from 1 Feb; last known 3 June √					
[Philadelphia] Aurora					from 8 Nov √	√	√	√	suspended 10 Sept; resumed 1 Nov √	√
[Philadelphia] Carey's U.S. Recorder									from 23 Jan to 30 Aug √	
[Philadelphia] Claypoole's Amer. D. Adv.							from 1 Jan √	√	√	√
[Philadelphia] Complete C. H. Companion	last known 30 Oct ×									
[Philadelphia] Constitutional Diary										from 2 Dec
[Philadelphia] Country Porcupine									from 5 Mar √	to 28 Aug √
[Philadelphia] Courier de l'Amerique			from 4 Dec √	(suspension) last known 22 Feb √						
[Philadelphia] Courrier de la France					first known 26 Apr √	from 15 Oct √	to 14 Mar √			
[Philadelphia] Courrier Français					last known 13 Feb ×	√	√	√	to 3 July √	
[Philadelphia] Courrier Politique				first known 19 Oct ×						
[Philadelphia] Daily Advertiser								from 7 Feb; last known 12 Sept √		
[Philadelphia] Dunlap's Amer. Daily Adv.		from 1 Jan √	√	suspended 14 Sept; resumed 2 Dec √	√	to 31 Dec √				
[Philadelphia] Federal Gazette	√	√	√	to 31 Dec √						
[Philadelphia] Finlay's American Reg.						from 25 Nov √	√	√	last known 1 May ×	
[Philadelphia] Freeman's Journal	√	√	to 16 May √							
[Philadelphia] Gales's Independent Gazr.							from 16 Sept √	to 12 Sept √		
Philadelphia Gazette					from 1 Jan √	√	√	√	√	√
[Philadelphia] Gazette of the United States	from 3 Nov √	√	√	suspended 18 Sept; resumed 11 Dec √	√	√	√	√	√	√
[Philadelphia] Gemeinnützige Phila. Cor.	last known 10 Aug ×									

Page 37   SYMBOLS: √ complete or extensive coverage exists   × few numbers known (usually less than 25% of those issued)   o no copies extant   Table for 1790–1799

Chronological Tables of American Newspapers 1690–1820

Table for 1790–1799

PENNSYLVANIA continued	1790	1791	1792	1793	1794	1795	1796	1797	1798	1799
[Philadelphia] General Advertiser	from 1 Oct ✓	✓	✓	suspended 27 Sept; resumed 23 Nov ✓	to 7 Nov ✓					
[Philadelphia] General-Postbothe	from 5 Jan to 29 June ✓									
[Philadelphia] Independent Gazetteer	✓	✓	✓	✓	✓	✓	to 10 Sept ✓			
[Philadelphia] Journal des Révolutions				from 25 Sept ✓	to 29 Jan ✓					
[Philadelphia] Level of Europe					from 1 Oct ✓		to 27 Jan ✓			
[Philadelphia] Mail		from 1 June ✓	✓	to 30 Sept ✓						
[Philadelphia] Merchants' Daily Advertiser								from 16 Jan ✓	to 30 June ✓	
Philadelphia Minerva						from 7 Feb ✓	✓	✓	to 7 July ✓	
[Philadelphia] National Gazette		from 31 Oct ✓	✓	to 26 Oct ✓						
[Philadelphia] Neue Phila. Correspondenz	first known 5 Oct ✓	✓	✓	suspended 4 Oct; resumed 22 Nov ✓	✓	✓	✓	✗	suspended 18 Sept; resumed 13 Nov ✓	suspended 27 Aug; resumed 22 Oct ✓
[Philadelphia] New World							from 15 Aug ✓	to 16 Aug ✓		
[Philadelphia] Pelosi's Marine List		first known 18 July ✓	last known 23 Apr ✗							
[Philadelphia] Pennsylvania Gazette	✓	✓	✓	✓	✓	✓	✓	✓	✓	✓
[Philadelphia] Pennsylvania Journal	✓	✓	✓	last known 18 Sept ✓						
[Philadelphia] Pennsylvania Mercury	✓	✓	to 1 Mar ✓							
[Philadelphia] Pennsylvania Packet	to 31 Dec ✓									
[Philadelphia] Pensy. Correspondenz									first known 2 Jan ✗	(suspension) last known 27 Dec ✗
[Philadelphia] Porcupine's Gazette								from 4 Mar ✓	✓	(after 28 Aug at Bustleton) to Oct 26 ✓
[Philadelphia] Radoteur				first & last known: 2 July & 3 Sept ✓						
[Philadelphia] Southwark Gazette								first & last known:25 July & 1 Aug ✓		
[Philadelphia] True American									from 2 July ✓	✓
[Philadelphia] Universal Gazette								only known 5 Jan		
[Philadelphia] Universal Gazette								from 16 Nov ✓	✓	✓

PENNSYLVANIA continued	1790	1791	1792	1793	1794	1795	1796	1797	1798	1799
Pittsburgh Gazette	√	o	o	√	√	√		√	√	√
Readinger Adler		o					(sample issue 29 Nov)	from 3 Jan √	√	√
[Reading] Impartial Reading Herald							(preliminary issue 22 June) from 22 July √	to 13 Jan √		
[Reading] Neue Unpartheyische R. Zeit.	√	√	√	√	√	√	√	√	√	√
[Reading] Weekly Advertiser							from 7 May √	√	√	√
Shippensburgh Messenger								only known 28 June		
Sunbury and Northumberland Gazette			first & last known: 23 June & 29 Dec x							
[Uniontown] Fayette Gazette									first known 10 Feb x	o
[Washington] Herald of Liberty										first known 28 Jan x
[Washington] Western Telegraphe						from 17 Aug √	√	√	x	o
West-Chester Gazette					only known 8 Jan					
Wilkesbarre Gazette								first known 5 Dec √	√	√
[Wilkesbarre] Herald of the Times							from 1 Nov √	to 31 Oct √		
[York] Pennsylvania Herald	√	√	√	√	x	x			√	last known 4 Sept x
[York] Unpartheyische York Gazette							first known 20 May √	√	x	o
[York] Volks-Berichter										from 25 July √
RHODE ISLAND										
[Newport] Companion									from 2 May √	to 20 July √
Newport Herald	√	last known 17 Sept √								
Newport Mercury	√	√	√	√	√	√	√	√	√	√
[Newport] Rhode-Island Museum					from 7 July; last known 29 Dec √					
Providence Gazette	√	√	√	√	√	√	√	√	√	√
Providence Journal										from 2 Jan √

SYMBOLS: √ complete or extensive coverage exists x few numbers known (usually less than 25% of those issued) o no copies extant Table for 1790–1799

Chronological Tables of American Newspapers 1690–1820

Table for 1790–1799

	1790	1791	1792	1793	1794	1795	1796	1797	1798	1799
RHODE ISLAND continued										
[Providence] State Gazette	✓									
[Providence] United States Chronicle		✓	✓	✓	✓	✓	from 4 Jan to 2 July ✓	✓	✓	✓
[Warren] Herald of the United States			from 14 Jan ✓	✓	✓	✓	✓	✓	✓	✓
SOUTH CAROLINA										
[Charleston] Carolina Gazette									from 1 Jan ✓	✓
[Charleston] City Gazette	✓	✓	✓	✓	✓	✓	✓	✓	✓	✓
[Charleston] Columbian Herald	×	×	×	✓	✓	✓	to 17 Dec ✓			
[Charleston] Daily Evening Gazette						first & last known: 10 Jan & 18 Feb ✓				
[Charleston] Evening Courier									from 31 July; last known 16 Nov ✓	
[Charleston] Patriote Français						only known 23 July				
[Charleston] South-Carolina State-Gazette					from 1 Jan ✓	✓	✓	✓	✓	✓
[Charleston] Star				first & last known: 12 July & 14 Sept ×						
[Charleston] State Gaz. of South-Carolina	✓	✓	✓	to 31 Dec ✓						
[Charleston] Telegraphe						first & last known: 16 Mar & 20 Mar ✓				
Columbia Gazette					(14 Jan extra) from 28 Jan; last known 8 Aug ×					
[Columbia] South Carolina Gazette			first known 10 July ✓	last known 3 Sept ×						
[Columbia] State Gazette						first known 23 Jan ×	✓	last known 1 Nov ×	×	
Georgetown Chronicle							first known 22 Mar ×			
Georgetown Gazette									from 8 May ✓	✓
[Georgetown] S.C. Independent Gazette		first known 21 May ×	last known 15 Sept ×							
TENNESSEE										
Knoxville Gazette		from 5 Nov ✓	✓	✓	✓	✓	×	✓	last known before suspension 2 Feb ×	(except 7 Aug none known in 1799)
[Knoxville] Impartial Observer										first known 11 Sept ×

	1790	1791	1792	1793	1794	1795	1796	1797	1798	1799
TENNESSEE continued										
Knoxville Register									first & last known: 14 Aug, & 30 Oct ✓	
Nashville Intelligencer										first & only other known: 17 July & 28 Aug
[Nashville] Rights of Man										only known 11 Mar
VERMONT										
[Bennington] Tablet of the Times								from 5 Jan to 31 Aug ✓		
[Bennington] Vermont Gazette	✓	✓	✓	✓	✓	✓	suspended 29 Dec ✓	resumed 5 Sept ✓	✓	✓
[Brattleboro] Federal Galaxy								from 6 Jan ✓	✓	✓
Burlington Mercury							first known 1 Apr ✓	last known 24 Mar ✓		
[Fair Haven] Farmer's Library						first known 3 Aug ✓	✓	(suspension in Mar–Nov) ✓	last known 3 Apr ×	
[Newbury] Orange Nightingale							first known 19 May ×	last known 4 Sept ×		
[Peacham] Green Mountain Patriot									from 23 Feb ✓	✓
[Putney] Argus								first known 16 Mar ✓	✓	last known 26 Feb ✓
[Rutland] Farmers' Library				from 1 Apr ✓	to 29 Nov ✓					
Rutland Herald					from 8 Dec ✓	✓	✓	✓	✓	✓
[Rutland] Herald of Vermont			from 25 June; last known 10 Sept ✓							
Vergennes Gazette									from 30 Aug (suspension in Nov) ✓	✓
[Westminster] Vermont Chronicle							from 4 July; last known 17 Oct ✓			
[Windsor] Morning Ray		first known 15 Nov ✓	last known 25 Sept ✓							
[Windsor] Vermont Journal	✓	✓	✓	✓	✓	✓	✓	✓	✓	✓
VIRGINIA										
[Alexandria] Columbian Mirror			from 21 Nov ✓	✓	×	✓	✓	✓	✓	✓
Alexandria Times								from 10 Apr ✓	✓	✓
[Alexandria] Virginia Gazette	✓	✓	×	last known 19 Sept ×						

SYMBOLS: ✓ complete or extensive coverage exists × few numbers known (usually less than 25% of those issued) o no copies extant   Table for 1790–1799

Chronological Tables of American Newspapers 1690–1820

Table for 1790–1799

VIRGINIA continued	1790	1791	1792	1793	1794	1795	1796	1797	1798	1799
[Dumfries] Republican Journal						first known 22 May ×	last known 3 Nov √			
[Dumfries] Virginia Gazette		from 29 Sept ×	×	last known 19 Dec ×						
[Fredericksburg] Genius of Liberty									first known 3 July ×	×
[Fredericksburg] Republican Citizen							first known 15 June √	last known 27 July √		
[Fredericksburg] Virginia Herald	√	√	√	√	√	√	√	√	√	√
Lynchburg and Farmer's Gazette					first known 5 Apr ×	(suspension) last known 28 Nov √				
[Lynchburg] Union Gazette					first & only other known: 18 & 25 Jan					
Lynchburg Weekly Gazette									first known 13 Oct ×	×
Lynchburg Weekly Museum								first known 21 Aug ×	last known 19 May ×	
[Norfolk] American Gazette			first known 10 Oct ×	×	×	√	√	last known 7 Nov ×		
Norfolk and Portsmouth Chronicle	×	√	last known 2 June ×							
[Norfolk] Epitome of the Times									first known 9 Apr ×	×
Norfolk Herald					first known 16 Aug √	√	√	√	√	√
[Norfolk] Virginia Chronicle			first known 28 July √	√	last known 19 Dec √					
Norfolk Weekly Journal								from 6 Sept √	to 19 Sept √	
[Petersburg] Independent Ledger				only known 8 May						
[Petersburg] Virginia Gazette	o	×	×	×	×	×	√	√	×	×
[Petersburg] Virginia Star						first & last known: 30 Apr & 16 July √				
Richmond and Manchester Advertiser						from 30 Apr √	last known 15 Nov √			
Richmond Chronicle						from 23 May √	to 27 Aug √			
[Richmond] Examiner									first known 6 Dec √	√
[Richmond] Observatory								first known 31 Aug ×	last known 26 Nov √	

VIRGINIA continued	1790	1791	1792	1793	1794	1795	1796	1797	1798	1799
[Richmond] Virginia Argus							from 19 Nov √	√	×	√
[Richmond] Virginia Federalist										first known 1 June √
[Richmond] Va. Gazette and General Adv.	from 25 Aug √	√	√	√	√	√	√	√	√	√
[Richmond] Va. Gazette and Public Adv.	×	×	×	to 16 Feb √						
[Richmond] Va. Gazette and R. & M. Adv.				from 15 Apr √	√	to 25 Apr √				
[Richmond] Va. Gazette & R. Chronicle				first known 6 Apr ×	√	to 19 May √				
[Richmond] Va. Gazette and R. Daily Adv.			from 1 Oct; last known 31 Dec √							
[Richmond] Va. Gazette and Weekly Adv.	×	×	×	√	×	√	√	last known 22 Apr √		
[Richmond] Va. Independent Chronicle	to 18 Aug √									
Staunton Gazette	only known 5 Feb									
[Staunton] Phenix									first known 12 Dec ×	×
Staunton Spy				first known 21 Sept ×	last known 1 Feb ×					
[Staunton] Virginia Gazette						first known 14 Feb ×	√	last known 20 Oct √		
[Winchester] Virginia Centinel	√	√	√	√	√	√	√	√	×	√
[Winchester] Virginia Gazette	√	last known 26 Nov √								
[Winchester] Willis's Virginia Gazette	first & last known: 3 Apr & 18 Sept √									
WEST VIRGINIA										
[Martinsburg] Berkeley Intelligencer										first known 29 May √
[Martinsburg] Potowmac Guardian			first known 3 Apr √	×	×	√	√	√	√	√
[Shepherdstown] Impartial Observer								first & only other known: 13 Sept & 11 Oct		
[Shepherdstown] Potowmac Guardian		first & last known: 27 June & 27 Dec ×								

SYMBOLS: √ complete or extensive coverage exists   × few numbers known (usually less than 25% of those issued)   o no copies extant

Table for 1790–1799

Chronological Tables of American Newspapers 1690–1820

CONNECTICUT	1800	1801	1802	1803	1804	1805	1806	1807	1808	1809
Bridgeport Advertiser							first known 5 June ×	×	×	last known 5 Jan
[Bridgeport] American Telegraphe	from 5 Nov ×	×	×	×	last known 6 June ×					
Bridgeport Herald						first known 7 Mar ×	last known 9 Jan ×			
[Bridgeport] Patriot of Seventy-Six					only known 1 Aug					
[Danbury] Connecticut Intelligencer										from 6 Dec ×
[Danbury] Farmers Journal	first known 14 Apr ×	√	×	last known 6 Sept √						
[Danbury] New-England Republican					from 18 July √	√	√	o	last known 16 Nov √	
[Danbury] Republican Farmer				from 16 Nov √	√	√	√	×	√	(suspension) last known 6 Sept √
[Danbury] Republican Journal	last known 10 Feb √									
[Danbury] Sun of Liberty	first known 1 July; to 8 Oct √									
[Hartford] American Mercury	√	√	√	√	√	√	√	√	√	√
[Hartford] Connecticut Courant	√	√	√	√	√	√	√	√	√	√
[Hartford] Connecticut Intelligencer					from 17 Mar; last known 8 May √					
[Hartford] Connecticut Mirror										from 10 July √
Litchfield Gazette									from 16 Mar √	to 17 May √
Litchfield Monitor	√	√	√	√	√	√	√	last known 29 July √		
[Litchfield] Witness						from 14 Aug √	√	(suspensions in May & June) to 24 June √	√	√
[Middletown] Middlesex Gazette	√	√	√	√	√	√	√	√	√	√
[New Haven] Belles-Lettres Repository									from 5 Mar; last known 16 Apr √	
[New Haven] Connecticut Herald				from 1 Nov √	√	√	√	√	√	√
[New Haven] Connecticut Journal	√	√	√	√	√	√	√	√	√	√
[New Haven] Conn. Post & N. H. Visitor			first & last known: 26 Oct. & 23 Nov √	from 3 Nov √	to 14 Nov √					
[New Haven] Herald of Minerva										

CONNECTICUT continued	1800	1801	1802	1803	1804	1805	1806	1807	1808	1809
[New Haven] Messenger	from 2 Jan √	suspended 2 Apr; resumed 29 Sept √	to 9 Aug √	. .	. .	. .	. .	. .	. .	. .
[New Haven] Sun of Liberty		from 26 Aug; last known 4 Nov √								
[New Haven] Visitor			from 30 Oct √	to 25 Oct √						
[New London] Bee	susp. 2 Apr (exc. 21 May); res. 27 Aug √	√	to 23 June √							
[New London] Connecticut Gazette	√	√	√	√	√	√	√	√	√	√
[New London] True Republican								from 1 July √	to 24 Feb √	
[New London] Weekly Oracle	√	last known 27 Oct √								
[Newfield] American Telegraphe	to 29 Oct √									
[Norwalk] American Apollo		from 12 Aug ×	last known 10 Mar ×							
[Norwalk] Independent Republican			from 17 June √	last known 6 Apr √						
[Norwalk] Sun of Liberty	from 21 Oct √	to 15 July √								
[Norwich] Connecticut Centinel			from 16 Feb √	√	√	√	√	last known 27 Oct √		
[Norwich] Courier	√	√	√	√	√	√	√	√	√	√
Norwich Packet	√	√	to 9 Feb √							
[Norwich] True Republican					from 20 June √	√	last known 5 Nov √			
[Sharon] Rural Gazette	first known 9 June ×	last known 13 July √								
[Stonington] America's Friend								first known 22 July √	last known 28 Sept √	
[Stonington] Impartial Journal	√	√	√	√	to 1 May √					
[Stonington-port] Patriot		from 24 July √	suspended 30 July √	resumed 11 Feb; none later known						
Windham Herald	√	√	√	√	√	×	√	×	√	×
DELAWARE										
[Dover] Constitutionalist					first known 6 Sept ×	last known 11 July ×				
[Dover] Federal Ark			from 14 Sept √	to 21 Feb √						

Page 45 SYMBOLS: √ complete or extensive coverage exists × few numbers known (usually less than 25% of those issued) o no copies extant Table for 1800–1809

Chronological Tables of American Newspapers 1690–1820

Table for 1800–1809

DELAWARE continued	1800	1801	1802	1803	1804	1805	1806	1807	1808	1809
Newcastle Argus						first & last known: 8 May & 9 Aug ✓				
[Wilmington] American Watchman										from 2 Aug ✓
[Wilmington] Delaware Gazette										from 8 July ✓
[Wilmington] Federal Ark				from 28 Feb ✓	last known 30 June ✓					
[Wilmington] Mirror of the Times	✓	✓	✓	✓	✓	✓	(suspensions in Apr–July) to 22 Aug ✓			
[Wilmington] Monitor	first known 8 Feb ×	×	(suspension) last known 1 Sept ×							
[Wilmington] Museum of Delaware					first known 8 Sept ×	×	○	✓	✓	last known 17 June ✓
DISTRICT of COLUMBIA										
[Georgetown] Cabinet	from 26 Aug (suspension in Nov) ✓	last known 6 Mar ×								
[Georgetown] Centinel & Country Gazette	last known 21 Mar ✓									
[Georgetown] Centinel of Liberty	to 14 Nov ✓									
[Georgetown] Columbian Repository				from 30 Sept ✓	last known 3 Feb ✓					
[Georgetown] Independent American										first known 26 Aug ✓
[Georgetown] Museum	from 18 Nov ✓	✓	to 22 Jan ✓							
[Georgetown] Museum; Georgetown Adv.										from 21 Jan; last known 10 Oct ✓
[Georgetown] Olio			from 1 July ✓	last known 4 Aug ✓						
[Georgetown] Washington Federalist	from 25 Sept ✓	✓	✓	✓	✓	✓	✓	×	✓	to 20 June ✓
Washington Advertiser	only known 20 Nov									
[Washington] American Literary Adv.			from 27 Mar ✓	✓	last known 20 Mar ×					
[Washington] Apollo			only known 1 May							
[Washington] Atlantic World								from 19 Jan; last known 31 Mar ✓		
Washington City Gazette	only known (specimen issue) 25 July									
Washington Expositor								first known 21 Nov ✓	✓	last known 6 Jan ✓

DIST. of COLUMBIA continued	1800	1801	1802	1803	1804	1805	1806	1807	1808	1809
[Washington] Monitor									from 12 May ✓	last known 20 June ✓
[Washington] National Intelligencer	from 31 Oct ✓	✓	✓	✓	✓	✓	✓	✓	✓	✓
[Washington] Spirit of 'Seventy-Six										first known 29 Dec ✓
[Washington] Universal Gazette	from 6 Nov ✓	✓	✓	✓	✓	✓	✓	✓	✓	✓
GEORGIA										
[Athens] Georgia Express									first known 23 July ✓	✓
Augusta Chronicle	✓	✓	✓	✓	✓	✓	✓	✓	✓	✓
[Augusta] Columbian Centinel					first known 3 July ×	o	✓	✓	×	✓
Augusta Herald	✓	✓	✓	✓	✓	✓	✓	✓	✓	✓
[Augusta] Mirror of the Times									first known 31 Oct ×	×
Louisville Gazette	✓		(suspension?) ✓	(suspension?) ✓	✓	×	×	×	o	o
[Louisville] Independent Register		only known 13 Aug								
[Milledgeville] Georgia Argus									first known 5 July ×	×
[Milledgeville] Georgia Journal										from 3 Nov ✓
Milledgeville Intelligencer									only known 22 Nov	
[Petersburg] Georgia & C. Gazette						first known 15 June ✓	last known 7 Aug ×			
[Savannah] Columbian Museum	✓	✓	✓	✓	✓	o	✓	✓	✓	✓
[Savannah] Federal Republican Advocate								first known 21 Sept ✓	last known 1 Feb ✓	
[Savannah] Georgia Gazette	✓	✓	to 25 Nov ✓							
[Savannah] Georgia Republican			from 21 Aug ✓	✓	✓	✓	✓	to 6 Mar ✓		
[Savannah] Public Intelligencer								first known 9 Apr ✓	✓	to 3 Feb ✓
[Savannah] Republican								from 10 Mar ✓	✓	✓
[Savannah] Southern Patriot					first known 14 Nov ✓	✓	✓	to 20 July ✓		

Page 47   SYMBOLS: ✓ complete or extensive coverage exists   × few numbers known (usually less than 25% of those issued)   o no copies extant   Table for 1800–1809

Chronological Tables of American Newspapers 1690–1820

GEORGIA continued	1800	1801	1802	1803	1804	1805	1806	1807	1808	1809
[Sparta] Farmer's Gazette				from 3 June √	√	√	√	last known 29 Aug √		
[Washington] Monitor						first known 23 Feb √	√	√	×	√
INDIANA										
[Vincennes] Indiana Gazette					first known 7 Aug √	×	last known 12 Apr ×			
[Vincennes] Western Sun								first known 11 July; susp. 3 Oct. to 17 Nov √	√	√
KENTUCKY										
[Bairdstown] Candid Review								first known 14 July ×	×	×
[Bardstown] Western American				from 6 Sept √	√	last known 17 May √				
[Danville] Informant						from 3 Sept √	√	last known 3 Mar ×		
[Danville] Mirror					from 3 Sept; only other known 24 Oct					
[Frankfort] Argus of Western America									from 27 Jan √	√
[Frankfort] Guardian of Freedom	(suspension) O	resumed 2 Oct √	√	√	√	last known 25 Mar √				
[Frankfort] Palladium	√	√	√	√	√	√	√	√	√	√
[Frankfort] Western World							from 7 July √	√	√	last known 26 July ×
[Lancaster] Political Theatre									first known 18 Nov √	
[Lexington] Independent Gazetteer				from 29 Mar √	√	last known 16 Nov √				
[Lexington] Kentucky Gazette	√	√	√	√	√	√	√	√	√	√
[Lexington] Reporter									from 12 Mar √	√
[Lexington] Stewart's Kentucky Herald	×	×	×	last known 2 Aug ×						
[Lincoln County] Lamp									only known 12 Jan	
[Louisville] Farmer's Library		first known 7 Dec ×	√	×	×	×	×	last known 23 July ×		
Louisville Gazette								first known 1 Dec √	×	×
[Louisville] Western American							first & last known: 6 Feb & 11 Sept √			

KENTUCKY continued

	1800	1801	1802	1803	1804	1805	1806	1807	1808	1809
[Paris] Kentucky Herald							from 17 Apr; only other known 8 May ✓			
[Paris] Stewart's Kentucky Herald						first known 25 Nov ✓	last known 27 Mar ✓			
[Paris] Western Citizen									first known 1 Sept ✗	○
[Russellville] Farmer's Friend										first known 2 Oct ✓
[Russellville] Mirror							from 1 Nov ✓	✓	✓	✗
[Washington] Republican Auxiliary								only known 15 Aug		
[Washington] Weekly Messenger				first & last known: 16 June & 6 Oct ✓						

LOUISIANA

	1800	1801	1802	1803	1804	1805	1806	1807	1808	1809
[New Orleans] Courrier de la Louisiane								from 14 Oct ✓	✓	✓
[New Orleans] Echo du Commerce									only known 28 Sept	
[New Orleans] Lanterne Magique									only known 20 Nov	
[New Orleans] Louisiana Gazette					from 24 July ✓	✓	✓	✓	✓	✓
[New Orleans] Misisipi									first & only other known: 12 Oct & 10 Dec	
[New Orleans] Moniteur de la Louisiane	✗	○	✓	✓	✗	✗	✓	✓	✓	✓
[New Orleans] Orleans Gazette					first known 22 Dec ✓	✓	✓	✓	✗	✗
[New Orleans] Telegraphe				first known 17 Dec ✗	✗	○	✗	✗	✗	✗
[New Orleans] Union				first known 20 Dec ✓	last known 28 Nov ✗					

MAINE

	1800	1801	1802	1803	1804	1805	1806	1807	1808	1809
[Augusta] Kennebec Gazette	from 14 Nov ✓				suspended 11 Feb-28 Mar & from 21 Nov ✓	resumed 16 Jan ✓	✓	✓	✓	✗
[Augusta] Kennebeck Intelligencer	to 6 June ✓									
[Buckstown] Gazette of Maine						from 25 July ✓	✓	✓	✓	✓
[Castine] Columbian Informer			from 22 Apr; last known 1 July ✓							
[Castine] Eagle										from 14 Nov ✓

Page 49   SYMBOLS: ✓ complete or extensive coverage exists   ✗ few numbers known (usually less than 25% of those issued)   ○ no copies extant   Table for 1800–1809

MAINE continued	1800	1801	1802	1803	1804	1805	1806	1807	1808	1809
Castine Journal	√	to 30 Oct √								
[Hampden] Penobscot Patriot				first & last known: 26 Feb & 26 Mar √						
[Kennebunk] Annals of the Times			from 1 July; last known 30 Sept √	from 13 Jan √	to 3 Jan					
[Kennebunk] Eagle of Maine						from 20 Mar to 31 July √				
Kennebunk Gazette										
[Kennebunk] Weekly Visiter										from 24 June √
Portland Commercial Gazette				from 16 Nov √	last known 30 Aug √					
[Portland] Eastern Argus		√	√	from 8 Sept √	√	√	√	√	√	√
[Portland] Eastern Herald	√	√	√	√	to 31 Dec √					
[Portland] Freeman's Friend								from 19 Sept √	suspended 13 Feb; resumed 21 May √	√
[Portland] Gazette	√	√	√	√	√	√	√	√	√	√
Portland Magazine						from 11 May; last known 8 June √				
[Portland] Oriental Trumpet	last known 5 Nov √									
[Saco] Freeman's Friend						from 21 Aug √	√	to 15 Aug √		
[Wiscasset] Eastern Repository				from 16 June √	√	×	×	last known 23 June ×		
[Wiscasset] Republican								first known 7 Oct √	last known 27 Jan ×	
MARYLAND										
Abingdon Patriot						only known 1 Oct				
[Annapolis] Maryland Gazette	√	√	√	√	√	√	√	√	√	√
[Annapolis] Maryland Republican										from 17 June √
[Baltimore] American	√	√	×	√	√	√	√	√	√	√
[Baltimore] American Patriot			from 4 Sept; suspension from 18 Dec √	to 11 Jan & 19 July to 6 Aug; last kn. 15 Oct √						
[Baltimore] Democratic Republican			first & last known: 17 Mar & 13 Aug √							

SYMBOLS: √ complete or extensive coverage exists   x few numbers known (usually less than 25% of those issued)   o no copies extant   Table for 1800–1809

MARYLAND continued	1800	1801	1802	1803	1804	1805	1806	1807	1808	1809
Baltimore Evening Post						from 25 Mar √	√	√	√	√
[Baltimore] Federal Gazette	√	√	√	√	√	√	√	√	√	√
[Baltimore] Federal Republican									from 4 July √	√
[Baltimore] North American									from 11 Jan √	to 3 Oct √
Baltimore Price-Current				from 14 Feb √	√	√	√	√	√	√
[Baltimore] Republican			from 1 Jan √	to 30 Dec √	("Valedictory Appendix" 14 Jan)					
Baltimore Telegraphe	√	√	√	√	√	√	√	last known 7 Feb √		
[Baltimore] Whig								first known 15 Oct √	(suspension) √	√
[Cumberland] American Eagle										only known 15 Feb
Cumberland Impartialist										only known 24 Jan
[Easton] Maryland Herald	√	√	√	√	to 13 Nov √					
[Easton] People's Monitor										from 4 Mar √
[Easton] Republican Star		o	√	√	√	√	√	√	√	√
[Elizabethtown] Maryland Herald	first known 11 Feb x	√	√	√	√	√	√	√	√	√
[Fredericktown] Bartgis's Federal Gazette	last known 23 Apr √									
[Fredericktown] Bartgis's Republican Gaz.		first known 11 Feb x	√	√	√	√	√	√	x	√
Frederick-Town Herald			from 19 June √	√	√	√	√	√	√	√
[Fredericktown] Hornet			from 22 June √	√	√	√	√	last known before suspension 23 June √		resumed 1 Feb √
[Fredericktown] Independent Amer. Vol.								from 8 July √	last known 28 Dec √	
[Fredericktown] Republican Advocate			from 6 Dec √	√	√	√	√	√	last known 15 Dec √	
[Fredericktown] Rights of Man	last known 5 Nov x									
Hagers-Town Gazette										first known 23 May √
[Hagerstown] Westliche Correspondenz	o	x	o	o	o	o	o	o	o	o

Chronological Tables of American Newspapers 1690–1820

	1800	1801	1802	1803	1804	1805	1806	1807	1808	1809
MARYLAND continued										
[Rockville] Maryland Register								first known 3 Apr	only other known 2 June	
MASSACHUSETTS										
[Boston] American Republican										from 13 Mar to 3 Apr √
[Boston] Columbian Centinel	√	√	√	√	√	√	√	√	√	√
[Boston] Columbian Detector									(prospectus issues 7 & 9 Nov) from 18 Nov √	to 19 May √
[Boston] Constitutional Telegraph	√	√	to 22 May √							
Boston Courier						from 13 June √	√	√	√	last known 4 May √
[Boston] Daily Advertiser										from 5 June; only other known 29 July
[Boston] Democrat					from 4 Jan √	√	√	√	√	last known 2 June √
Boston Gazette	from 9 Oct √	√	√	√	√	√	√	√	√	√
[Boston] Gazetteer				from 2 Apr to 31 Dec √						
[Boston] Independent Chronicle	√	√	√	√	√	√	√	√	√	√
[Boston] Massachusetts Mercury	√	√	√	to 8 Mar √						
Boston Mirror									from 22 Oct √	√
[Boston] New-England Palladium				from 11 Mar √	√	√	√	√	√	√
Boston Patriot										from 3 Mar √
[Boston] Repertory					from 3 Feb √	√	√	√	√	√
[Boston] Republican Gazetteer			from 26 May √	to 30 Mar √						
[Boston] Russell's Gazette	to 6 Oct √									
[Boston] Times								from 12 Dec √	to 15 Oct √	
[Brookfield] Political Repository	√	√	to 4 May √							
[Dedham] Columbian Minerva	√	√	√	√	to 4 Sept √					
[Dedham] Norfolk Repository						from 14 May; suspended 17 Sept √	resumed 25 Mar √	√	√	to 28 Dec √

MASSACHUSETTS continued

	1800	1801	1802	1803	1804	1805	1806	1807	1808	1809
Greenfield Gazette	√	√	√	√	√	√	√	√	√	√
[Haverhill] Merrimack Intelligencer									from 2 July √	√
Haverhill Museum	from 5 Dec √	√	√	√	to 27 Nov √					
[Haverhill] Observer					from 4 Dec √	√	to 22 Nov √			
[Lenox] Watch Light										first & last known: 27 Mar & 15 May √
[Leominster] Telescope	from 2 Jan √	√	to 14 Oct √							
[Leominster] Weekly Messenger							first & last known: 6 Feb & 18 Dec √			
[New Bedford] Columbian Courier	√	√	√	√	√	to 1 Mar √				
New-Bedford Mercury								from 7 Aug √	√	√
[New Bedford] Old Colony Gazette		from 4 June; last known 30 July √							from 21 Oct √	√
[Newburyport] American Intelligencer								from 7 Apr; last known 18 Sept √		
Newburyport Gazette										
Newburyport Herald	√	√	√	√	√	√	√	√	√	√
[Newburyport] Merrimack Gazette				from 21 Mar √	last known 11 Feb √					
[Newburyport] Merrimack Magazine						from 17 Aug √	last known 9 Aug √			
[Newburyport] New-England Repertory				from 6 July √	to 21 Jan √					
[Newburyport] Political Calendar					from 26 Mar √	last known 17 June √				
[Newburyport] Statesman									from 15 Aug √	last known 9 Mar √
[Northampton] Anti-Monarchist									from 14 Dec √	√
[Northampton] Hampshire Gazette	√	√	√	√	√	√	√	√	√	√
[Northampton] Hive	to 23 June √									
[Northampton] Patriotic Gazette				from 23 Aug √	√	to 29 Jan √				
[Northampton] Republican Spy					from 3 July √	√	√	√	to 16 Nov √	

Page 53   SYMBOLS: √ complete or extensive coverage exists   × few numbers known (usually less than 25 % of those issued)   o no copies extant   Table for 1800–1809

Chronological Tables of American Newspapers 1690–1820

Table for 1800–1809

MASSACHUSETTS continued	1800	1801	1802	1803	1804	1805	1806	1807	1808	1809
[Pittsfield] Berkshire Gazette	last known 11 Feb √									
[Pittsfield] Berkshire Reporter								first known 17 Jan √	√	√
[Pittsfield] Sun	from 16 Sept √	√	√	√	√	√	√	√	√	√
[Salem] Essex Register								from 23 July √	√	√
[Salem] Friend								from 3 Jan to 18 July √		
Salem Gazette	√	√	√	√	√	√	√	√	√	√
[Salem] Impartial Register	from 12 May √	to 31 Dec √								
Salem Register			from 4 Jan √	√	√	(except 29 July) √	√	to 16 July √		
[Salem] Weekly Visitant							from 1 Jan to 27 Dec √			
[Springfield] Federal Spy	√	√	√	√	√	to 31 Dec √				
[Springfield] Hampshire Federalist							from 7 Jan √	√	√	√
[Springfield] Republican Spy				from 14 June √	to 11 June √					
[Stockbridge] Farmer's Herald									from 30 July √	×
[Stockbridge] Political Atlas								from 14 Feb √	to 22 July √	
[Stockbridge] Western Star	√	√	√	√	√	×	last known 8 Nov ×			
[Worcester] Independent Gazetteer	from 7 Jan √	to 29 Dec √								
[Worcester] Massachusetts Spy	√	√	√	√	√	√	√	√	√	√
[Worcester] National Aegis		from 2 Dec √	√	√	√	suspended 11 Dec √	resumed 19 Feb √	√	√	√
[Worcester] Scorpion										from 26 July to 9 Aug √
MICHIGAN										
[Detroit] Michigan Essay										only known 31 Aug
MISSISSIPPI										
[Natchez] Constitutional Conservator				only known 16 Apr						

Table for 1800–1809

MISSISSIPPI continued	1800	1801	1802	1803	1804	1805	1806	1807	1808	1809
Natchez Gazette										from 7 Jan / to 16 Nov √ (suppl. 19 Nov).
[Natchez] Green's Impartial Observer	from 5 May √	last known 4 Apr ×								
[Natchez] Intelligencer		first & last known: 22 Sept. & 8 Dec ×								
[Natchez] Mississippi Gazette		first & last known: 13 Oct & 1 Dec √								
[Natchez] Mississippi Herald			first known 10 Aug ×	×			√	to 31 Dec √		
[Natchez] Mississippi Messenger					from 7 Sept √	√	√	√	last known 11 Aug √	
[Natchez] Mississippian									first known 8 Dec √	×
[Natchez] Weekly Chronicle									from 6 July √	√
MISSOURI										
[St. Louis] Missouri Gazette									first known 26 July √	√
NEW HAMPSHIRE										
[Amherst] Farmer's Cabinet			from 11 Nov √	√	√	√	√	√	√	√
[Amherst] Village Messenger	√	to 5 Dec √								
[Concord] American Patriot	√	√	√	√	√			√	√	to 11 Apr √
[Concord] Courier of New Hampshire		√	√	√	√	to 30 Oct √				
Concord Gazette							first known 19 July √	suspended 17 Feb; resumed 9 June √	√	√
[Concord] New-Hampshire Patriot										from 18 Apr √
[Concord] Republican Gazette		from 5 Feb √	√	last known 28 Apr √						
[Dover] Sun	√	√	√	√	√	√	√	√	√	√
Gilmanton Gazette	first & last known: 6 Dec & 20 Dec √									
Gilmanton Rural Museum	last known 28 Feb ×									
[Hanover] Dartmouth Gazette	√	√	√	√	√	√	√	√	√	√
[Haverhill] Coos Courier									from 21 Apr √	√

Page 55 SYMBOLS: √ complete or extensive coverage exists × few numbers known (usually less than 25 % of those issued) o no copies extant

Chronological Tables of American Newspapers 1690–1820

Table for 1800–1809

NEW HAMPSHIRE continued	1800	1801	1802	1803	1804	1805	1806	1807	1808	1809
[Keene] New Hampshire Sentinel	√	√	√	√	√	√	√	√	√	√
[Portsmouth] Federal Observer	last known 29 May √									
[Portsmouth] Herald of Gospel Liberty									from 1 Sept √	√
[Portsmouth] Intelligencer							from 4 Dec √	×	×	×
[Portsmouth] New-Hampshire Gazette	√	√	√	√	√	√	√	√	√	√
Portsmouth Oracle				from 22 Oct √	√	√	√	√	√	√
[Portsmouth] Oracle Post				from 25 Oct √	√	to 18 June √				
[Portsmouth] Political Star					from 28 June; last known 8 Nov √					
[Portsmouth] Republican Ledger	√	√	√	last known 20 Dec √						
[Portsmouth] United States Oracle	from 4 Jan √	√	√	to 18 Oct √						
[Walpole] Farmer's Weekly Museum	√	√	√	√	√	√	√	suspended 27 Mar √	resumed 24 Oct √	√
[Walpole] Political Observatory				from 19 Nov √	√	√	√	√	√	last known 13 Mar √
NEW JERSEY										
[Bridgeton] Apollo					first known 21 June; to 6 Dec √					
[Elizabeth Town] Federal Republican				first & only other known: 21 & 28 June						
[Elizabeth Town] New-Jersey Journal	√	√	√	√	√	√	√	√	√	√
[Hackensack] Impartial Register					first known 13 Nov ×	last known 15 May ×				
[Morristown] Genius of Liberty	√	√	√	√	√	√	×	×	×	√
[Morristown] Palladium of Liberty									from 31 Mar √	√
[New Brunswick] Guardian	√	√	√	√	√	√	√	√	×	×
[Newark] Centinel of Freedom	√	√	√	√	√	√	√	√	√	(except 21 Mar) √
Newark Gazette	√	√	√	√	last known 18 Dec √					
[Newark] Modern Spectator								from 27 Nov √	to 25 Nov √	

NEW JERSEY continued	1800	1801	1802	1803	1804	1805	1806	1807	1808	1809
[Newark] New-Jersey Telescope									from 4 Nov √	to 7 Nov √
[Newark] Republican Herald										
[Trenton] Federalist	√	√	√	√	only known 25 Dec	√	√	√	√	√
[Trenton] Miscellany						from 10 June; last known 2 Dec √				
[Trenton] New-Jersey State Gazette	to 1 July √									
[Trenton] True American		from 10 Mar √	√	√	√	√	√	√	√	√
NEW YORK										
[Albany] Balance										from 4 Jan √
Albany Centinel	√	√	√	√	√	√	last known 31 Oct √			
Albany Gazette	√	√	√	√	√	√	×	√	√	×
[Albany] Guardian								from 21 Nov √	to 12 Nov √	
Albany Register	√	√	√	√	√	√	√	√	√	√
[Albany] Republican Crisis							from 11 Nov √	√	to 27 Dec √	
[Athens] Monitor							only known 8 Feb			
Aurora Gazette						first known 17 July √	×	×	last known 17 June	
[Ballston Spa] Independent American									from 27 Sept √	√
[Ballston Spa] Republican Telescope		first & only other known: 16 & 23 Apr								
[Ballston Spa] Saratoga Advertiser					from 12 Nov √	√	o	o	×	
[Batavia] Cornucopia										first known 12 May ×
[Batavia] Genesee Intelligencer								first & last known: 20 May & 15 July √		
Brooklyn Intelligencer								first & last known: 23 July & 24 Sept √		
[Brooklyn] Long Island Courier		√	√	to 13 Jan √						
[Brooklyn] Long Island Star										from 8 June √

Page 57   SYMBOLS: √ complete or extensive coverage exists   × few numbers known (usually less than 25% of those issued)   o no copies extant   Table for 1800–1809

Chronological Tables of American Newspapers 1690–1820

Table for 1800–1809

NEW YORK continued	1800	1801	1802	1803	1804	1805	1806	1807	1808	1809
[Brooklyn] L. I. Weekly Intelligencer							from 3 July √	last known 11 June ×		
Brooklyn Minerva								from 21 Oct; last known 9 Dec √		
Cambridge Gazette					first & only other known: 21 Mar & 2 May					
[Canandaigua] Genesee Messenger							from 25 Nov √	√	√	√
[Canandaigua] Ontario Freeman				first known 29 Dec	(suspension in Oct) ×	resumed 4 June; last known 6 Aug √				
[Canandaigua] Ontario Gazette	×	×	last known 7 Dec ×							
[Canandaigua] Ontario Repository										from 25 Apr √
[Canandaigua] Western Repository				from 3 May √	√	√	×	√	√	to 8 Apr √
[Catskill] American Eagle									first known 3 Aug ×	√
Catskill Recorder					from 14 May √	√	√	√	√	√
[Catskill] Western Constellation	from 26 May √	√	√	√	last known 9 Apr ×					
[Cazenovia] Pilot									from 10 Aug √	√
Cooperstown Federalist										from 3 June √
[Cooperstown] Impartial Observer									from 22 Oct √	to 27 May √
[Cooperstown] Otsego Herald	√	√	√	√	√	√	√	√	√	√
[Geneva] Expositor							from 19 Nov √	√	√	to 14 June √
Geneva Gazette										from 21 June √
[Geneva] Imparial American		last known 17 Feb √								
[Goshen] Friend of Truth				only known 25 Jan						
[Goshen] Orange County Gazette						first known 29 May ×	×	×	×	×
[Goshen] Orange County Patriot					first & last known: 1 Feb & 8 Dec ×					
[Goshen] Orange Eagle										from 7 Feb √
[Goshen] Orange Patrol	from 7 Jan ×	√	last known 20 Apr ×							

NEW YORK continued	1800	1801	1802	1803	1804	1805	1806	1807	1808	1809
[Herkimer] Bunker-Hill										first known 30 Nov √
[Herkimer] Farmer's Monitor						from 29 Jan √		to 19 May √		
Herkimer Herald									first known 26 July ×	last known 2 Nov ×
[Herkimer] Pelican					last known 12 Nov ×			first known 8 June √	last known 20 June ×	
[Herkimer] Telescope			O	O						
[Hudson] Balance		from 21 May √		√	√	√	√	√	to 27 Dec √	
[Hudson] Bee			from 17 Aug √	√	√	√	√	√	√	√
Hudson Gazette	O	√		to 27 Dec √						
[Hudson] Northern Whig										from 3 Jan √
[Hudson] Republican Fountain								first & last known: 22 Jan & 26 Mar √		
[Hudson] Wasp			from 7 July √	to 26 Jan √						
[Johnstown] Montgomery Intelligencer							first & last known: 9 June & 4 Aug √			
[Johnstown] Montgomery Monitor										first known 6 Dec √
[Johnstown] Montgomery Republican										first known 2 May ×
[Kingston] Plebeian				first known 3 Aug √	√	√	√	√	√	√
[Kingston] Ulster County Gazette	×	×	×	last known 30 Apr ×						
[Kingston] Ulster Gazette				first known 13 Aug ×	×	×	×	×	×	×
[Lansingburgh] Farmers' Register				first known 8 Feb √	√	√	√	to 10 Nov √		
Lansingburgh Gazette	√	√	√	√	√	√	√	√		√
[Manlius] Herald of the Times									first known 19 July ×	last known 31 Jan ×
Manlius Times										first known 18 July ×
[Mount Pleasant] Impartial Gazetteer	only known 22 July									
[New York] American Citizen	from 10 Mar √	√	√	√	√	√	√	√	√	√

Page 59   SYMBOLS: √ complete or extensive coverage exists   × few numbers known (usually less than 25 % of those issued)   O no copies extant   Table for 1800–1809

Chronological Tables of American Newspapers 1690–1820

Table for 1800–1809

NEW YORK continued	1800	1801	1802	1803	1804	1805	1806	1807	1808	1809
[New York] Argus	to 8 Mar √									
New-York Aurora								first known 26 May √	√	last known 7 June ×
[New York] Chronicle Express			from 25 Nov √	√	last known 21 May √					
[New York] Columbian										from 1 Nov √
[New York] Columbian Herald									first & last known: 2 Jan & 27 Feb √	
[New York] Commercial Advertiser	√	√	√	√	√	√	√	√	√	√
[New York] Corrector					from 28 Mar; last known 26 Apr √					
[New York] Daily Advertiser	√	√	√	√	√	√	to 30 Aug √			
[New York] Daily Advertiser								from 4 Aug to 31 Dec √		
[New York] Daily Advertiser									from 12 Sept √	last known 1 June ×
New-York Evening Post		from 16 Nov √	√	√	√	√	√	√	√	√
[New York] Forlorn Hope	from 24 Mar; last known 13 Sept √									
New-York Gazette	√	√	√	suspended 25 Aug; resumed 24 Oct √	√	√	√	√	√	√
[New York] Greenleaf's New York Journal	to 8 Mar √									
New-York Herald			from 2 Jan √	√	√	√	√	√	√	√
[New York] Independent Republican							from 25 Nov √	last known 6 May √		
New-York Journal			from 22 May; last known 14 Aug ×							
New York Journal										from 10 June √
[New York] Mercantile Advertiser	√	√	√	√	√	√	√	√	√	√
[New York] Moniteur Français					only known 29 Nov					
[New York] Morning Chronicle			from 1 Oct √	√	√	√	√	to 15 June √		
[New York] Observateur Impartial									only known 6 Feb	
[New York] Observer										from 19 Feb; suspended 6 Aug √

NEW YORK continued	1800	1801	1802	1803	1804	1805	1806	1807	1808	1809
[New York] Oracle									from 1 Jan to 10 Sept √	
[New York] Pelican									from 6 Oct; only other known 12 Nov	
[New York] People's Friend							from 1 Sept √	to 31 Dec √		
[New York] Porcupine's Gazette	only issued 13 Jan									
New-York Price-Current		√	√	√	√	√	√	√	√	√
[New York] Prisoner of Hope	from 3 May to 23 Aug √									
[New York] Public Advertiser								from 5 Jan √	√	√
[New York] Remembrancer						only known 1 June				
[New York] Republican Watch-Tower	from 12 Mar √	√	√	√	√	√	√	√	√	√
[New York] Spectator	√	√	√	√	√	√	√	√	√	√
[New York] Spirit of '76										from 7 Mar; last known 27 Apr √
New-York Spy	from 8 Nov √	to 7 Feb √								
[New York] Temple of Reason			only known 8 May							
[New York] Washington Republican										from 29 July ×
[New York] Weekly Inspector							from 30 Aug √	to 22 Aug √		
New-York Weekly Museum	√	√	√	suspended 13 Apr; resumed 5 Nov √	√	√	√	√	√	√
[New York] Weekly Visitor			from 9 Oct √	suspended 27 Aug; resumed 29 Oct √	√	suspended 1 Oct; resumed 2 Nov √	√	to 24 Oct √		
[Newburgh] Political Index							from 1 May √	√	√	
[Newburgh] Recorder of the Times				first known 29 June √	√	√	last known 24 Apr √			
[Newburgh] Rights of Man	first known 14 Apr ×	×	×	×	√	√	last known 13 Mar √			
[Norwich] Olive Branch										to 13 Nov √
[Owego] American Constellation						o				
[Owego] American Farmer				first known 14 Sept √	×	o	o	×	×	×

Page 61   SYMBOLS: √ complete or extensive coverage exists   × few numbers known (usually less than 25% of those issued)   o no copies extant   Table for 1800–1809

Chronological Tables of American Newspapers 1690–1820

Table for 1800–1809

NEW YORK continued	1800	1801	1802	1803	1804	1805	1806	1807	1808	1809
[Oxford] President									first & only other known: 2 Apr & 19 June.	
[Peterboro] Freeholder								first known 18 Feb ×	×	×
[Plattsburgh] American Monitor										from 4 Aug √
[Poughkeepsie] American Farmer	to 22 July √									
[Poughkeepsie] Farmer							from 15 Apr √	last known 10 Feb √		
[Poughkeepsie] Farmers' & Mechanics' Rep.										only known 25 Nov
[Poughkeepsie] Guardian		first known 15 Dec √	to 1 June √							
Poughkeepsie Journal	√	×	√	√	√	√	√	√	√	√
[Poughkeepsie] Political Barometer			from 8 June √	√	√	√	√	√	√	√
[Rome] Columbian Patriotic Gazette	√	√	last known 6 Sept ×							
[Sag Harbor] Suffolk County Herald			from 19 June √	last known 3 Jan						
[Sag Harbor] Suffolk Gazette					from 20 Feb √	suspended 19 Aug; resumed 16 Sept √	√	√	√	√
[Salem] Northern Centinel	×	√	×	√	to 15 May √					
[Salem] Northern Post					first known 29 May √	√	√	√	√	
[Salem] Washington Register					first known 7 Feb ×	×	×	○	×	
Schenectady Gazette	×									
[Schenectady] Mohawk Advertiser								first known 7 Aug √	×	×
[Schenectady] Western Budget								first known 25 July ×	○	×
[Schenectady] Western Spectator				first known 21 Apr ×	×	×	○	last known 25 Apr ×		
[Schoharie] American Herald										first known 18 Aug √
[Scipio] Western Luminary		first & last known: 7 Apr & 21 July ×								
[Sherburne] Olive Branch							from 21 May √	√	to 6 Feb √	

NEW YORK continued	1800	1801	1802	1803	1804	1805	1806	1807	1808	1809
[Sherburne] Western Oracle					first & last known: 3 May & 12 July √					
Somers Museum										from 8 Nov √
[Troy] Farmers' Register								first known 1 Dec √	√	√
Troy Gazette	√		from 15 Sept √	√	√	√	√	√	√	√
[Troy] Northern Budget		√	√	√	√	√	√	√	√	√
[Union] American Constellation	first known 22 Nov ×	last known 3 Oct √								
[Utica] Columbian Gazette				first known 28 Mar √	√	√	√	√	√	√
[Utica] Patriot				from 28 Feb √	√	√	√	√	√	√
[Utica] Whitestown Gazette	×	√	√	to 21 Feb √						
[Wardsbridge] Orange County Republican							from 6 May √		last known 23 Mar ×	
Waterford Gazette		first known 17 Nov √	√	√	√	√	o	×	×	×
Watertown Herald										only known 3 Apr
NORTH CAROLINA										
[Edenton] Encyclopedian Instructor	only known 21 May									
Edenton Gazette	from 19 Nov ×	last known 9 Apr ×								
Edenton Gazette							first known 26 Feb ×	√	√	√
[Edenton] Post-Angel	first & only other kn.: 10 Sept & 12 Nov									
Elizabeth-City Gazette								from 31 July ×	last known 14 Jan ×	
[Fayetteville] North–Carolina Intelligencer							first known 18 Jan ×	×	last known 17 June ×	
[Halifax] North–Carolina Journal	√	√	√	×	×	suspended 5 Aug; resumed. 30 Sept √	√	√	×	×
[New Bern] Carolina Federal Republican										first known 12 Jan ×
Newbern Gazette	×	×	o	×	last known 9 Mar ×					
Newbern Herald										first known 20 Jan √

Page 63   SYMBOLS: √ complete or extensive coverage exists   × few numbers known (usually less than 25 % of those issued)   o no copies extant   Table for 1800–1809

Chronological Tables of American Newspapers 1690–1820

Table for 1800–1809

NORTH CAROLINA continued	1800	1801	1802	1803	1804	1805	1806	1807	1808	1809
[New Bern] Morning Herald								first known 17 Sept ×	last known 30 Dec ×	
[New Bern] North Carolina Circular				first known 23 Sept ×	×	last known 10 July ×				
[Raleigh] Minerva				from 2 May √	√	√	√	√	√	√
[Raleigh] North-Carolina Minerva	√	√	√	to 25 Apr √						
Raleigh Register	√	√	√	√	√	√	√	√	√	√
[Raleigh] Star									from 3 Nov √	√
[Salisbury] North-Carolina Mercury	√	last known 13 Aug √								
Washington Gazette				only known 2 Nov						
[Wilmington] Cape-Fear Herald								first known 24 July ×	last known 29 Nov ×	
Wilmington Gazette	√		√	√	√	√	√	√	×	×
[Wilmington] True Republican										from 3 Jan; last known 7 Nov √
OHIO										
[Chillicothe] Fredonian	first & last known: 11 July, & 26 Sept √									
[Chillicothe] Freeman's Journal								from 19 Feb √	last known 5 Aug ×	
[Chillicothe] Independent Republican										from 8 Sept √
[Chillicothe] Ohio Herald						from 27 July √	last known 15 Nov ×			
[Chillicothe] Scioto Gazette	from 10 Oct √	√	√	√	√	√	√	√	√	√
[Chillicothe] Supporter									from 6 Oct √	√
[Cincinnati] Liberty Hall					from 4 Dec √	√	√	√	√	√
[Cincinnati] Western Spy	suspended 16 Apr; resumed 21 May √	suspended 10 June; resumed 24 June √	√	√	√	√	√	√	√	(suspension in Apr) O
[Cincinnati] Whig										from 13 Apr ×
Dayton Repertory									first known 30 Sept; suspended. last known 21 Oct √	resumed 1 Feb; Sept; suspended. last known 14 Dec √
[Lancaster] Western Oracle								first & last known: 6 Feb & 29 May √		

OHIO continued	1800	1801	1802	1803	1804	1805	1806	1807	1808	1809
[Lebanon] Western Star								from 13 Feb ×	×	×
[Marietta] Commentator								from 16 Sept ×	(suspension) ×	×
[Marietta] Ohio Gazette			first known 1 Jan ×	o	o	×	×	×	√	×
[New Lisbon] Ohio Patriot										first known 18 Nov √
[St. Clairsville] Impartial Expositor										only known 25 Mar
[Steubenville] Western Herald							first known 16 Aug √	√	√	o
PENNSYLVANIA										
[Allentown] Northampton Adverteiser									first known 11 June √	last known 8 Sept ×
[Beavertown] Minerva								from 4 Nov ×	×	o
Bedford Gazette						from 21 Sept √	√	√	√	o
[Carlisle] Cumberland Register						from 20 Sept √	√	√	√	√
[Carlisle] Eagle	first known 10 Sept	only other known 4 Nov								
Carlisle Gazette	√	√	√	√	√	√	√	√	√	√
Carlisle Herald			from 1 July √	√	√	√	√	√	o	o
[Carlisle] Unpartheyische Americaner										first known 13 Sept ×
[Chambersburg] Franklin Repository	×	×	o	o	√	√	√	√	√	√
[Chambersburg] Pennsylvania Republican									only known 2 Mar	
[Downingtown] American Republican										from 1 Aug √
[Downingtown] Temperate Zone									first known 19 July ×	to 25 July ×
[Doylestown] Farmer's Weekly Journal	first & last known: 18 Nov. & 30 Dec √									
[Doylestown] Pennsylvania Correspondent					from 7 July √	√	√	√	√	√
[Easton] American Eagle	√	√	√	√	√	last known 2 Nov √	√	×	×	
Eastoner-Deutsche Patriot						from 13 Feb √	√	×	×	o

SYMBOLS: √ complete or extensive coverage exists × few numbers known (usually less than 25 % of those issued) o no copies extant

Table for 1800–1809

Chronological Tables of American Newspapers 1690–1820

Table for 1800–1809

PENNSYLVANIA continued	1800	1801	1802	1803	1804	1805	1806	1807	1808	1809
[Easton] Neuer Unpartheyischer E. Bothe	○	○	○		√	to 6 Feb √				
[Easton] Northampton Correspondent							from 25 Jan √	√	○	○
[Easton] Northampton Farmer						from 21 Dec √	√	√	√	○
[Easton] Pennsylvania Herald									from 10 Aug √	√
[Erie] Mirror	first known 19 Nov √								from 26 May to 19 Nov √	√
[Gettysburg] Adams Centinel		√	√	√	√	√	√	√	√	√
Gettysburg Gazette				from 21 Jan; last known 19 Aug √						
[Gettysburg] Sprig of Liberty					from 27 Jan √	√	√	last known 23 Jan √		
[Greensburg] Farmers Register		√	√	√	√	√	✗	✗	✗	√
[Harrisburg] Dauphin Guardian						from 1 June √	√	✗	√	√
[Harrisburgh] Farmers Instructor	from 8 Jan √	√	to 5 May √							
Harrisburger Morgenröthe Zeitung	√	√	√	√	√	√	√	√	√	√
[Harrisburgh] Oracle of Dauphin	√	√	√	√	√	√	√	√	√	√
[Harrisburgh] Times								from 21 Sept √	suspended 28 Mar √	√
Huntingdon Gazette			first known 29 Apr ✗	✗	○	✗	√	√	√	√
[Huntingdon] Guardian of Liberty	only known 14 Aug √									
[Lancaster] Americanische Staatsbothe	first known 29 Jan √	√	√	√	√	√	√	√	√	√
[Lancaster] Constitutional Democrat						first known 9 July √	√	last known 1 Dec √		
Lancaster Correspondent				to 6 Sept √						
[Lancaster] Hive				from 22 June √	√	to 12 June √				
[Lancaster] Intelligencer	√	√	√	√	√	√	√	√	√	√
Lancaster Journal	√	√	√	√	√	√	√	√	√	√
Lancaster Repository							first & last known: 23 Aug. & 13 Dec √			

PENNSYLVANIA continued	1800	1801	1802	1803	1804	1805	1806	1807	1808	1809
[Lancaster] Times									from 8 Apr ✓	✓
[Lancaster] Volksfreund									from 9 Aug ✓	✓
[Lancaster] Wahre Amerikaner					from 10 Nov ✓	✓	✓	✓	✓	✓
[Lebanon] Freymüthige Libanoner								from 1 Jan ✓	to 30 Nov ✓	
[Lebanon] Libanoner Morgenstern									from 7 Dec ✓	✓
[Lebanon] Weltbothe										first & last known: 14 Feb & 5 Sept ✓
[Lewistown] Western Star		first known 12 Feb ×				last known 23 Sept ×				
[Meadville] Crawford Weekly Messenger										✓
[Newtown] Farmers' Gazette							first known 17 Oct ×	×	×	last known 10 Nov ×
Norristown Gazette	to 6 June ✓									
Norristown Herald	from 10 Oct ✓	✓	✓	✓	✓	✓	✓	✓	✓	✓
Norristown Register				from 22 Sept ✓	✓	to 14 Mar ✓				
[Norristown] True Republican		first known 2 Jan ×	×	last known 6 May ✓						
[Norristown] Weekly Register						from 21 Mar ✓	✓	✓	✓	✓
[Northumberland] Republican Argus			from 24 Dec ✓	✓	✓	✓	✓	suspended 11 Mar; resumed 3 June ✓	✓	✓
[Northumberland] Sunbury & N. Gazette	×	×	o	×	×	×	o	×	×	o
[Philadelphia] Amerikanischer Beobachter									from 9 Sept ✓	✓
[Philadelphia] Aurora	✓	✓	✓	✓	✓	✓	✓	✓	✓	✓
[Philadelphia] Claypoole's Amer. D. Adv.	to 30 Sept ✓									
[Philadelphia] Constitutional Diary	last known 3 Feb ✓									
[Philadelphia] Democratic Press								from 27 Mar ✓	✓	✓
[Philadelphia] Evening Post					from 20 Feb to 11 June ✓					
[Philadelphia] Freeman's Journal					from 12 June ✓	✓	✓	✓	✓	✓

Page 67   SYMBOLS: ✓ complete or extensive coverage exists   × few numbers known (usually less than 25% of those issued)   o no copies extant   Table for 1800–1809

Chronological Tables of American Newspapers 1690–1820

Table for 1800–1809

PENNSYLVANIA continued	1800	1801	1802	1803	1804	1805	1806	1807	1808	1809
Philadelphia Gazette	√	√	to 31 Dec √							
[Philadelphia] Gazette of the United States	√	√	√	√	to 18 Feb √					
[Philadelphia] Hope's Phila. Price-Current					first known 3 Dec ×	√	√	√	√	√
[Philadelphia] Independent Whig			first & last known: 20 Mar. & 4 Aug ×							
[Philadelphia] Library					from 25 Feb √	last known 22 June √				
[Philadelphia] Literary Intelligencer								only known 1 May		
[Philadelphia] Philadelphia Literary Reporter										first & last known: Jan & Sept √
[Philadelphia] Neue Phila. Correspondenz	√	o	×	√	√	√	√	√	√	last known 26 Dec √
[Philadelphia] Pelican						from 28 Oct √	×	last known 21 Feb √		
[Philadelphia] Pennsylvania Democrat										from 11 Aug √
[Philadelphia] Pennsylvania Gazette	√	√	√	√	√	√	√	×	×	×
[Philadelphia] Political & Commercial Reg.					from 2 July √	√	√	√	√	√
[Philadelphia] Poulson's Amer. Daily Adv.	from 1 Oct √	√	√	√	√	√	√	√	√	√
[Philadelphia] Relfs Philadelphia Gazette				from 1 Jan √	√	√	√	√	√	√
[Philadelphia] Relf's Phila. Prices Current		only known 31 Oct								
Philadelphia Repository	from 15 Nov √	√	suspended 7 Aug; resumed 2 Oct √	√	to 29 Dec √					
[Philadelphia] Spirit of the Press						from 14 Sept √	√	√	×	×
[Philadelphia] Supporter	first & last known: 15 Apr. & 10 Nov √									
[Philadelphia] Temple of Reason		from 22 Apr √	√	last known 19 Feb √						
[Philadelphia] Tickler								from 16 Sept √	(suspensions) √	
[Philadelphia] True American	√	√	√	√	√	√	√	√	√	√
[Philadelphia] United States' Gazette					from 20 Feb √	√	√	√	√	√
[Philadelphia] Universal Gazette	to 11 Sept √									

PENNSYLVANIA continued	1800	1801	1802	1803	1804	1805	1806	1807	1808	1809
[Philadelphia] Weekly Monitor					from 16 June to 8 Dec √					
[Pittsburgh] Commonwealth						from 24 July √	√	√	√	√
Pittsburgh Gazette	√	√	√	√	√	o	√	√	√	√
[Pittsburgh] Tree of Liberty	from 16 Aug √	√	√	√	√	√	×	√	×	last known 6 Dec ×
[Presque Isle] Mirror									from 26 Nov √	√
Readinger Adler	√	√	√	√	√	√	√	√	√	√
[Reading] Neue Unpartheyische R. Zeit.	√	√	last known 1 Sept √							
[Reading] Weekly Advertiser	√	√	√	√	√	√	√	√	√	√
[Sunbury] Freiheitsvogel	only known 24 Dec									
[Uniontown] Fayette Gazette	×	×	o	last known 29 July ×						
[Uniontown] Genius of Liberty						first known 15 Mar ×	×	×	×	×
[Washington] Herald of Liberty	o	last known 14 Sept ×								
[Washington] Reporter									from 15 Aug √	√
[Washington] Western Telegraphe	×	o	×	×	×	×	×	×	×	o
[West Chester] Chester & Del. Federalist										first known 15 June √
Wilkesbarre Gazette	√	last known 20 July ×								
[Wilkesbarre] Luzerne County Federalist		from 5 Jan √	√	√	√	√	√	√	√	√
[Williamsport] Lycoming Gazette								first known 22 Jan √	√	√
York Recorder	from 29 Jan √	√	√	√	√	√	×	×	×	×
[York] Unpartheyische York Gazette	×	o	o	o						
[York] Volks-Berichter	√	√	last known 25 Feb ×							
[York] Wahre Republicaner						first known 17 July ×	o	×	o	o

Page 69   SYMBOLS: √ complete or extensive coverage exists   × few numbers known (usually less than 25% of those issued)   o no copies extant   Table for 1800–1809

Chronological Tables of American Newspapers 1690–1820

Table for 1800–1809

RHODE ISLAND	1800	1801	1802	1803	1804	1805	1806	1807	1808	1809
[Bristol] Mount Hope Eagle								from 10 Jan ✓	last known 8 Oct ×	
[Newport] Guardian of Liberty	from 3 Oct ✓	to 26 Sept ✓								
Newport Mercury	✓	✓	✓	✓	✓	✓	✓	✓	✓	✓
[Newport] Rhode-Island Republican		from 3 Oct ✓	✓	✓	✓	✓	to 26 June ✓			
[Newport] Rhode-Island Republican										from 22 Mar ✓
[Providence] American									from 21 Oct ✓	to 17 Oct ✓
[Providence] Columbian Phenix									from 16 Jan ✓	✓
Providence Gazette	✓	✓	✓	✓	✓	✓	✓	✓	✓	✓
[Providence] Impartial Observer	from 4 Aug ✓	suspended 26 Jan; resumed 14 Mar ✓	to 6 Mar ✓							
Providence Journal	✓	to 30 Dec ✓								
Providence Phoenix			from 11 May ✓	✓	✓	✓	✓	✓	to 9 Jan ✓	
[Providence] Rhode-Island American										from 20 Oct ✓
[Providence] Rhode-Island Farmer					from 9 Aug ✓	to 31 Jan ✓				
[Providence] United States Chronicle	✓	✓	✓	✓	to 17 May ✓					
[Warren] Bristol County Register										from 11 Mar ✓
[Warren] Herald of the United States	✓	✓	✓	✓	✓	×	✓	✓	×	×
SOUTH CAROLINA										
[Charleston] Carolina Gazette	✓	✓	✓	✓	✓	✓	✓	✓	✓	✓
[Charleston] Carolina Weekly Messenger							first known 18 July ✓	✓	✓	✓
[Charleston] City Gazette	✓	✓	✓	✓	✓	✓	✓	✓	✓	✓
Charleston Courier				from 10 Jan ✓	✓	✓	✓	✓	✓	✓
[Charleston] Echo du Sud		first & last known: 22 June. & 15 July ✓								
[Charleston] Federal Carolina Gazette	from 2 Jan; last known 25 Dec ×									

SOUTH CAROLINA continued	1800	1801	1802	1803	1804	1805	1806	1807	1808	1809
[Charleston] Oracle	√							from 1 Jan; last known 8 Dec √		
[Charleston] South-Carolina State-Gazette		√	last known 20 Sept √							
Charleston Spectator							from 21 June; last known 5 Dec √			
[Charleston] Strength of the People										from 24 June √
[Charleston] Times	from 6 Oct √	√	√	√	√	√	√	√	√	√
[Columbia] State Gazette	×	√	×	√	√	√	√	×	×	o
Georgetown Gazette	√	√	×	o	×	o	×	×	×	o
[Pendleton] Miller's Weekly Messenger								first known 20 Mar √	√	o
TENNESSEE										
Carthage Gazette									from 13 Aug ×	√
[Carthage] Western Express									only known 21 Nov	
[Greeneville] Tennessee Express						only known 5 July				
[Jonesborough] Newspaper & Wash. Adv.				first known 5 Nov ×	last known 15 Feb ×					
Knoxville Gazette		first known after suspension 7 Jan ×	×	×	×	×	×	last known 13 Nov ×		
[Knoxville] Impartial Observer	last known 10 Sept (extra) √									
[Knoxville] Western Centinel										first known 11 Mar ×
[Knoxville] Wilson's Knoxville Gazette							first known 6 Dec ×	×	√	√
[Nashville] Clarion									first known 16 Feb ×	o
[Nashville] Impartial Review						from 13 Dec ×	√	√	√	last known 16 Mar ×
[Nashville] Review										first known 10 Nov √
[Nashville] Tennessee Gazette	first known 25 Feb √	√	√	√	√	√	last known 9 Aug (extra) ×			
VERMONT										
[Bennington] Epitome of the World								from 10 Feb to 12 Oct √		

SYMBOLS: √ complete or extensive coverage exists   × few numbers known (usually less than 25% of those issued)   o no copies extant   Table for 1800–1809

Chronological Tables of American Newspapers 1690–1820

Table for 1800–1809

VERMONT continued	1800	1801	1802	1803	1804	1805	1806	1807	1808	1809
[Bennington] Green-Mountain Farmer										from 17 Apr √
[Bennington] Ploughman		first known 27 July √	to 1 Feb √							
[Bennington] Vermont Gazette	suspended 9 Jan; resumed 6 Mar √	(suspension in Mar) √	√	suspended 3 Jan; resumed 6 Apr √	(suspension in Nov) √	√	√	suspended 3 Feb √		
[Bennington] World							√	from 19 Oct √	√	last known 27 Mar √
[Brattleboro] Federal Galaxy	√		√	last known 17 Jan √						
[Brattleboro] Independent Freeholder									from 3 Dec √	last known 8 Apr √
[Brattleboro] Reporter				from 21 Feb √	√	×	√	×	√	×
[Burlington] Vermont Centinel		from 19 Mar √	√	√	√	×	√	√	√	√
[Chester] Green Mountain Palladium								from 22 June √	last known 12 Apr ×	
[Danville] North Star								from 8 Jan √	√	√
Middlebury Mercury		from 16 Dec √	√	√	√	√	√	√	√	√
[Montpelier] Freemen's Press										from 25 Aug √
[Montpelier] Vermont Precursor							from 22 Nov √	to 13 Nov √		
[Montpelier] Watchman								from 20 Nov √	√	×
[Peacham] Green Mountain Patriot	√			√	√	√	√	last known before suspension: 26 May √		
[Randolph] Weekly Wanderer		first known 24 Jan √	√	√	√	√	√	√	√	√
Rutland Herald	√	√	√	√	√	√	√	√	√	√
[Rutland] Vermont Courier									from 25 July √	√
[Rutland] Vermont Mercury			first known 29 Mar √	√	last known 12 Mar √					
St. Albans Adviser									first & last known: 31 Mar. & 21 July √	
[St. Albans] Champlain Reporter										first known 11 May ×
Vergennes Gazette	√	last known 8 Oct √								
Windsor Federal Gazette		from 3 Mar √	√	√	to 25 Dec √					

VERMONT continued	1800	1801	1802	1803	1804	1805	1806	1807	1808	1809
[Windsor] Post-Boy						from 1 Jan ✓	✓	to 31 Mar ✓		
[Windsor] Vermont Journal	✓	✓	✓	✓	✓	✓	✓	✓	✓	✓
[Windsor] Vermont Republican										from 2 Jan ✓
[Woodstock] Northern Memento						from 16 May; last known 14 Nov ✓				
VIRGINIA										
Alexandria Advertiser	from 8 Dec ✓	✓	✓	✓	✓	✓	✓	✓	to 9 July ✓	
[Alexandria] Columbian Advertiser			from 2 Aug; last known 22 Nov ✓							
[Alexandria] Columbian Mirror	last known 6 Dec ✓									
Alexandria Expositor			from 26 Nov ✓	✓	✗	✓	✗	last known 1 June ✗		
Alexandria Gazette									from 11 July ✓	✓
Alexandria Times	only known 5 Dec	✓	to 31 July ✓							
[Fincastle] Herald of Virginia		first & last known: 8 May & 10 July ✓								
Fincastle Weekly Advertiser				first known 7 Sept ✓	last known 18 Feb ✓					
[Fredericksburg] Apollo	first known 24 Oct ✓	last known 13 Nov ✓								
[Fredericksburg] Courier										
[Fredericksburg] Genius of Liberty	last known 22 July ✗									
Fredericksburgh News-Letter		only known 25 May								
[Fredericksburg] Virginia Express				first known 19 May ✓	✓	last known 28 Mar ✗				
[Fredericksburg] Virginia Herald	✓	✗	✓	✓	✓	✓	✓	✓	✓	✓
[Leesburg] True American	only known 30 Dec									
[Lexington] Rockbridge Repository		first known 21 Aug ✗	(suspension in Aug?) O	first known after suspension 25 Oct ✓	✗	last known 6 Aug ✗				
[Lexington] Virginia Telegraphe				first known 15 Feb ✓	last known before suspension 8 Oct ✓		resumed 23 Aug ✓	✓	last known 3 Feb ✗	
Lynchburg Gazette					only known 22 Feb					

Page 73   SYMBOLS: ✓ complete or extensive coverage exists   × few numbers known (usually less than 25 % of those issued)   o no copies extant   Table for 1800–1809

Chronological Tables of American Newspapers 1690–1820

Table for 1800–1809

VIRGINIA continued	1800	1801	1802	1803	1804	1805	1806	1807	1808	1809
Lynchburg Press										first known 13 May ×
Lynchburg Star							first known 27 Feb √	√	○	×
Lynchburg Weekly Gazette	×	last known 2 May ×								
[Newmarket] Virginische Volksberichter								(preliminary issue 7 Oct) from 16 Dec √	√	last known 14 June √
[Norfolk] Commercial Register			from 16 Aug √	to 11 Jan √						
[Norfolk] Epitome of the Times	×	√	last known 30 Mar √							
Norfolk Gazette	√	√	√	√	from 17 July √	√	√	√	√	√
Norfolk Herald	√	√	√	√	×	×	×	×	×	×
Petersburg Intelligencer	first known 17 June ×	×	√	√	√	√	√	√	√	×
[Petersburg] Republican	first known 12 June ×	√	(suspension in July–Sept)	√	√	√	√	×	×	×
[Petersburg] Virginia Apollo								from 15 Apr to 30 May √		
[Petersburg] Virginia Gazette	last known 1 Apr ×									
[Petersburg] Virginia Mercury								first known 13 May ×	last known 10 Feb ×	
[Richmond] Enquirer					from 9 May √	√	√	√	√	√
[Richmond] Examiner	√	√	√	√	to 10 Jan √					
[Richmond] Friend of the People	first & last known: 16 May & 5 July √									
[Richmond] Impartial Observer							from 1 May √	(suspension) last known 2 July √		
[Richmond] Press	first & only other known: 31 Jan & 7 Feb									
[Richmond] Recorder		first known 8 Aug ×	√	last known 24 Aug √						
[Richmond] Spirit of 'Seventy-Six									from 13 Sept √	last known 4 Nov ×
[Richmond] Virginia Argus	√	√	√	√	√	√	√	√	√	√
[Richmond] Virginia Federalist	last known 2 Aug √									
[Richmond] Va. Gazette and General Adv.	√	√	√	√	√	√	√	√	√	to 19 Dec √

VIRGINIA continued	1800	1801	1802	1803	1804	1805	1806	1807	1808	1809
[Richmond] Virginia Patriot										from 26 Dec √
[Richmond] Virginian									from 1 Jan; last known 8 Nov √	
[Richmond] Visitor										from 11 Feb √
[Staunton] Candid Review						first known 18 Jan ×	o	last known 18 Sept ×		
[Staunton] Deutsche Virginier Adler										only known 18 Nov
Staunton Eagle								first known 14 Aug √	√	×
[Staunton] Phenix	o	o	o	×	last known 5 Sept ×					
Staunton Political Censor									first known 22 June √	last known 22 Feb ×
[Staunton] Political Mirror	first known 3 June ×	last known 29 Sept √								
[Winchester] Democratic Lamp										first & only other kn.: 22 Aug & 21 Nov
[Winchester] Independent Register					first & last known: 25 Sept. & 20 Nov √					
[Winchester] Philanthropist							first known 25 Mar ×	×	×	last known 28 Feb ×
Winchester Triumph of Liberty		first known 13 May		only other known 29 Nov						
[Winchester] Virginia Centinel	√	√	√	o	o	×	×	×	×	×
WEST VIRGINIA										
[Charlestown] Farmer's Repository									from 1 Apr √	√
[Martinsburg] Berkeley Intelligencer	×	×	o	o	o	o	√	last known 23 Oct ×		
[Martinsburg] Potowmac Guardian	last known 2 Apr ×									
[Martinsburg] Republican Atlas	from 16 Apr ×	last known 4 Nov ×								
[Morgantown] Monongalia Gazette										only known 8 Sept
Wheeling Repository								from 5 Mar √	to 5 Nov √	

SYMBOLS: √ complete or extensive coverage exists × few numbers known (usually less than 25% of those issued) o no copies extant   Table for 1800–1809

Chronological Tables of American Newspapers 1690–1820

ALABAMA	1810	1811	1812	1813	1814	1815	1816	1817	1818	1819
Blakeley Sun									from 12 Dec √	last known 2 June √
Cahawba Press and Alabama Intelligencer										first known 10 July ×
[Claiborne] Alabama Courier										from 19 Mar ×
[Fort Stoddert] Mobile Centinel		first known 30 May	only other known 29 Jan							
[Huntsville] Alabama Republican								first known 15 July √	√	√
Huntsville Gazette							only known 21 Dec			
[Huntsville] Madison Gazette				first known 19 Oct ×	×		last known 27 Feb ×			
Mobile Gazette				first known 23 July (extra) ×	○	○	○	○	×	suspended 22 Sept; resumed 27 Oct √
[St. Stephens] Halcyon						first known 2 June (extra) ×	○	○	○	√
ARKANSAS										
[Arkansas Post] Arkansas Gazette										from 20 Nov √
CONNECTICUT										
[Bridgeport] Connecticut Courier					first known 3 Aug ×	×	×	×	×	×
Bridgeport Gazette	first known 27 June ×	last known 9 Jan ×								
[Bridgeport] Republican Farmer	from 25 Apr √	√	×	√	√	√	√	×	×	×
[Danbury] Connecticut Intelligencer	last known 7 Nov ×									
[Danbury] Day			first & last known: 19 May & 15 Dec ×							
Danbury Gazette				first known 3 Aug √	last known 29 Mar √					
[Hartford] American Mercury	√	√	√	√	√	√	√	√	√	√
[Hartford] Connecticut Courant	√	√	√	√	√	√	√	√	√	√
[Hartford] Connecticut Mirror	√	√	√	√	√	√	√	√	√	√
[Hartford] Times								from 1 Jan √	√	√
Litchfield Journal									first & last known: 8 Apr & 20 Oct √	

CONNECTICUT continued	1810	1811	1812	1813	1814	1815	1816	1817	1818	1819
Litchfield Republican										first known 19 May ✓
[Middletown] Connecticut Spectator					from 20 Apr ✓	✓	last known 10 Apr ✓			
[Middletown] Middlesex Gazette	✓	✓	✓	✓	✓	✓	✓	✓	✓	✓
[New Haven] Columbian Register			from 1 Dec ✓	✓	✓	✓	✓	✓	✓	✓
[New Haven] Connecticut Herald	✓	✓	✓	✓	✓	✓	✓	✓	✓	✓
[New Haven] Connecticut Journal	✓	✓	✓	✓	✓	✓	✓	✓	✓	✓
[New London] Connecticut Gazette	✓	✓	✓	✓	✓	✓	✓	✓	✓	✓
[New London] Republican Advocate									first known 15 Apr ✓	✓
Norwalk Gazette									from 6 May ✓	✓
[Norwich] Courier	✓	✓	✓	✓	✓	✓	✓	✓	✓	✓
[Norwich] Native American			from 4 Mar ✓	to 23 June ✓						
[Windham] Advertiser									first known 7 May ✓	last known 11 Mar ✓
Windham Herald	✓	✓	✓	✓	✓	suspended 30 Mar; resumed 27 July ✓	to 19 Sept ✓			
[Windham] Register								first & last known: 13 Mar. & 11 Dec ×		
DELAWARE										
[Wilmington] American Watchman	from 21 Sept; last known 27 Oct ✓	✓	✓	✓	✓	✓	✓	✓	✓	✓
[Wilmington] Delaware Freeman	last known 30 June ✓									
[Wilmington] Delaware Gazette										
[Wilmington] Delaware Gazette					from 19 Apr ✓	✓	✓	✓	✓	✓
[Wilmington] Delaware Patriot							from 9 July; last known 4 Oct ✓			
[Wilmington] Delaware Statesman		from 10 July ✓	✓	last known 24 July ×						
DISTRICT of COLUMBIA										
[Georgetown] Daily Federal Republican					from 4 Jan ✓	✓	to 3 Apr ✓			

Page 77   SYMBOLS: ✓ complete or extensive coverage (usually less than 25% of those issued)   o no copies extant   × few numbers known   Table for 1810–1819

Chronological Tables of American Newspapers 1690–1820

Table for 1810–1819

DIST. of COLUMBIA continued	1810	1811	1812	1813	1814	1815	1816	1817	1818	1819
[Georgetown] Federal Republican		first known 3 Aug √	√	√	√	√	to 2 Apr √			
[Georgetown] Independent American	last known 29 Dec √									
[Georgetown] Messenger							from 17 Apr √	to 24 Oct √		
[Georgetown] National Messenger								from 27 Oct √	√	√
[Georgetown] Spirit of 'Seventy-Six		from 22 Feb ×	√	(suspended late in year)	(resumed in Feb) last known 4 Mar ×					
Washington City Gazette					first & last known: 17 Jan & 17 Dec √					
[Washington] City of Washington Gazette								first known 12 Nov √	√	√
Washington City Weekly Gazette						from 25 Nov √	√	to 18 Oct √		
[Washington] Daily National Intelligencer				from 1 Jan √	√	√	√	√	√	√
[Washington] National Intelligencer	√	√	√	√	√	√	√	√	√	√
[Washington] Spirit of 'Seventy-Six	√	last known 15 Feb √								
[Washington] Universal Gazette	√	√	√	√	to 13 May √					
GEORGIA										
Athens Gazette	√	×	√	√	from 17 Feb √	√	√	×	×	×
[Athens] Georgia Express				to 13 Aug √						
Augusta Chronicle	√	√	√	√	√	√	√	√	√	√
[Augusta] Columbian Centinel	×	(suspension) last known 14 Oct ×								
[Augusta] Georgia Advertiser										first known 12 May ×
[Augusta] Georgia Gazette							first & last known: 5 Feb & 11 Mar √			
Augusta Herald	√	×	√	√	√	√	√	√	√	×
[Augusta] Mirror of the Times	×	last known 28 Oct ×								
Darien Gazette										first known 4 Jan ×
[Louisville] American Advocate							first & last known: 22 Feb & 28 Nov √			

GEORGIA continued	1810	1811	1812	1813	1814	1815	1816	1817	1818	1819
[Louisville] American Standard			only known 14 May							
Louisville Courier		from 21 Aug; last known 30 Oct √								
Louisville Gazette	×	last known 2 Mar √								
[Milledgeville] Georgia Argus	√	×			×	o	to 14 Feb √			
[Milledgeville] Georgia Journal	√	√	√	√	√	√	√	√	√	√
[Milledgeville] Georgia Republican										only known 28 Sept
[Milledgeville] Reflector								from 12 Nov √	√	last known 2 Feb √
Milledgeville Republican							first & only other known: 20 & 27 Mar			
[Savannah] American Patriot			from 14 Apr to 5 June √							
[Savannah] Columbian Museum	√	√	√	×	√	×	o	√	√	√
Savannah Gazette								from 14 Jan to 30 Jan √		
[Savannah] Georgian									from 25 Nov	√
[Savannah] Morning Chronicle									first known 8 May ×	last known 28 June ×
Savannah Price Current									first known 21 Nov √	×
[Savannah] Republican	√	√	√	√	√	√	√	√	√	√
[Washington] Friend and Monitor						from 13 Jan; last known 22 Dec √				
[Washington] Monitor	√	×	×	√	×	to 6 Jan (extra)				
[Washington] News							first known 23 Feb ×	×	o	×
ILLINOIS										
Edwardsville Spectator										from 29 May √
[Kaskaskia] Illinois Herald					only known 13 Dec					
[Kaskaskia] Illinois Intelligencer									from 27 May √	√
[Kaskaskia] Western Intelligencer							first known 15 May √	√	to 20 May √	

Page 79   SYMBOLS: √ complete or extensive coverage exists   × few numbers known (usually less than 25% of those issued)   o no copies extant   Table for 1810–1819

Chronological Tables of American Newspapers 1690–1820

Table for 1810–1819

	1810	1811	1812	1813	1814	1815	1816	1817	1818	1819
ILLINOIS continued										
[Shawneetown] Illinois Emigrant									first known 17 June ×	(suspensions) to 18 Sept √
[Shawneetown] Illinois Gazette										from 25 Sept √
INDIANA										
Brookville Enquirer										from 5 Feb √
[Brookville] Plain Dealer							first & only other known: 5 & 12 Nov			
[Corydon] Indiana Gazette								first known 15 Feb ×	○	√
[Jeffersonville] Indianian										first known 13 Nov √
[Lawrenceburg] Dearborn Gazette									only known 17 Aug	
[Lawrenceburg] Indiana Oracle										first known 29 Sept √
[Lexington] Cornucopia of the West							only known 8 June			
[Lexington] Western Eagle						from 8 July √	to 6 Jan			
[Madison] Indiana Republican								first known 16 Jan √	√	√
[Madison] Western Eagle				from 26 May √	last known 8 Apr √					
[Salem] Tocsin									first known 31 Mar ×	×
[Vevay] Indiana Register							first known 8 July ×	last known 25 Nov ×		
[Vincennes] Indiana Centinel								from 14 Mar ×	○	√
[Vincennes] Western Sun	suspended 27 Oct; resumed 8 Dec √	suspended 5 Jan to 15 June & 3 Aug to 9 Nov √	suspended 22 Feb; resumed 7 Mar √	susp. 20 Mar to 10 July & 30 Oct to 11 Dec √	√	suspended 16 Sept; resumed 16 Dec √	√	√	√	suspended 20 Feb; resumed 20 Mar √
KENTUCKY										
[Bairdstown] Candid Review	last known 27 Aug ×									
Bardstown Repository					first known 29 June ×	×	×	○	○	×
[Cynthiana] Guardian of Liberty								first known 11 Jan; suspended 27 Dec √	resumed 7 Mar √	last known 13 Mar √
[Danville] Impartial Observer	first known 10 Dec ×	last known 22 Jan √								
[Danville] People's Friend										only known 30 Jan

KENTUCKY continued	1810	1811	1812	1813	1814	1815	1816	1817	1818	1819
[Frankfort] American Republic	from 26 June ✓	✓	last known 17 Apr ✓							
[Frankfort] Argus of Western America	✓	✓	✓	✓	✓	✓	✓	✓	✓	✓
[Frankfort] Commentator								first known 17 Jan ×	×	✓
[Frankfort] Palladium	✓	✓	✓	✓	×	×	last known 6 Sept ×			
[Frankfort] Western World	last known 8 June ✓									
[Georgetown] Minerva					first known 14 May	only other known 18 Feb				
Georgetown Patriot							from 20 Apr ✓	last known 10 May ×		
[Georgetown] Telegraph		first known 25 Sept ×	o	last known 22 Dec ×						
[Glasgow] Kentucky Patriot									only known 30 Sept	
[Glasgow] Patriot					only known 18 July					
[Harrodsburg] Light House						only known complete issue 27 May				
[Harrodsburg] National Pulse							first known 7 Dec ×	to 8 Nov ×		
[Hopkinsville] Western Eagle				only known 12 Feb						
[Lexington] American Statesman		from 20 July ✓	×	last known 30 Oct ×						
[Lexington] Castigator										first known 14 Apr ×
[Lexington] Imparial Observer	first known 15 Sept; to 17 Nov ✓									
[Lexington] Kentucky Gazette	✓	✓	✓	✓	✓	✓	✓	✓	✓	✓
[Lexington] Reporter	✓	✓	✓	✓	✓	✓	✓	✓	✓	✓
[Lexington] Western Monitor					from 3 Aug ✓	✓	✓	✓	✓	✓
Louisville Correspondent				first known 13 Jan ×	✓	✓	✓	last known 28 June ✓		
Louisville Gazette	o	last known 15 Mar ×								
[Louisville] Kentucky Herald									first known 22 July ×	×
[Louisville] Public Advertiser									from 30 June ✓	✓

Page 81   SYMBOLS: ✓ complete or extensive coverage exists   × few numbers known (usually less than 25 % of those issued)   o no copies extant   Table for 1810–1819

Chronological Tables of American Newspapers 1690–1820

Table for 1810–1819

	1810	1811	1812	1813	1814	1815	1816	1817	1818	1819
KENTUCKY continued										
[Louisville] Western Courier			first known 28 Aug √	√	√	√	√	×	○	○
[Maysville] Eagle						first known 3 Mar ×	×	√	×	○
[Paris] Instructer									only known 2 May	
[Paris] Western Citizen	×	×	√	√	√	√	√	√	√	×
[Richmond] Globe	first & last known: 24 Jan & 17 Oct ×									
[Richmond] Luminary		first known 14 Aug ×	×	○	×	○	×	○	○	○
[Russellville] Farmer's Friend	last known 14 Dec ×									
[Russellville] Mirror	○	○	last known 29 Jan ×							
[Russellville] Sovereign People				only known 24 Nov						
[Russellville] Weekly Messenger										first known 26 Jan √
[Shelbyville] Impartial Compiler										first of two issues known 30 Apr
[Washington] Dove	first known 17 Feb		only other known 21 Mar							
[Washington] Union					first known 8 Mar √	√	√	√	○	○
Winchester Advertiser					from 5 Aug √	last known 14 June √				
[Winchester] Kentucky Advertiser						first known 2 Aug √	√	last known before suspension 19 July √	first known after suspension 13 June ×	last known 30 Oct ×
LOUISIANA										
[Alexandria] Louisiana Herald										first known 20 Mar ×
[Alexandria] Louisiana Planter	only known 15 May									
[Alexandria] Louisiana Rambler									first & only other known: 28 Mar & 11 Apr.	
[Alexandria] Red-River Herald				only known 10 Sept						
Baton-Rouge Gazette				only known 19 June						first known 5 June ×
[Natchitoches] El Mexicano										
[New Orleans] Ami des Lois	first known 2 Jan √	√	√	√	√	√	√	√	√	√

LOUISIANA continued	1810	1811	1812	1813	1814	1815	1816	1817	1818	1819
New-Orleans Chronicle									first known 14 July ×	last known 14 Sept ×
[New Orleans] Courrier de la Louisiane	√	√	√	√	√	√	√	√	√	√
[New Orleans] Louisiana Gazette	√	√	√	√	√	√	√	√	√	√
[New Orleans] Mensagero Luisianes		first known 23 Mar ×								
[New Orleans] Moniteur de la Louisiane	√	√	√	√	last known 2 July √					
[New Orleans] Orleans Gazette	×	×	×	o	×	×	×	√	×	√
[New Orleans] Telegraphe	×	×	last known 18 Apr ×							
[New Orleans] Trumpeter			only known 10 Oct							
[St. Francisville] Louisianian									from 8 May (suspension in July–Sept.)	√
[St. Francisville] Time Piece		first known 25 Apr √	×	×	×	last known 17 Jan (extra) ×				
MAINE										
[Augusta] Herald of Liberty	from 13 Feb √	√	×	×	×	last known 2 Sept ×				
[Augusta] Kennebec Gazette	to 6 Feb ×									
Augusta Patriot								from 7 Mar; last known 15 Aug √		
Bangor Weekly Register						from 25 Nov √	√	suspended 23 Aug; resumed 25 Dec ×	×	×
[Buckstown] Gazette of Maine			last known 17 Apr √							
[Castine] Eagle	√	to 14 Dec √	19 Mar (extra)							
Eastport Sentinel									from 31 Aug ×	√
[Hallowell] American Advocate	from 23 Jan √	√	√	√	√	√	√	√	√	√
Hallowell Gazette					from 23 Feb √	√	√	√	√	√
[Kennebunk] Weekly Visiter	√	√	√	√	√	√	√	√	√	√
[Portland] Eastern Argus	√	√	√	√	√	√	√	√	√	√
[Portland] Freeman's Friend	to 9 June √									

SYMBOLS: √ complete or extensive coverage exists   × few numbers known (usually less than 25% of those issued)   o no copies extant   Table for 1810–1819

Chronological Tables of American Newspapers 1690–1820

Table for 1810–1819

	1810	1811	1812	1813	1814	1815	1816	1817	1818	1819
MAINE continued										
[Portland] Gazette	from 27 Apr √	√	√	√	√	√	√	√	√	√
[Portland] Herald of Gospel Liberty		to 21 June √								
MARYLAND										
[Annapolis] Maryland Gazette	√	√	√	√	√	√	√	√	√	√
[Annapolis] Maryland Republican	√	√	√	√	√	√	√	√	√	√
[Baltimore] American	√	√	√	√	√	√	√	√	√	√
[Baltimore] American Farmer										from 2 Apr √
Baltimore Evening Post	√	to 22 June √								
[Baltimore] Federal Gazette	√	√	√	√	√	√	√	√	√	√
[Baltimore] Federal Republican	√	√	suspended 22 June √				resumed 4 Apr √	√	√	
[Baltimore] Journal of the Times									from 12 Sept √	to 6 Mar √
[Baltimore] Maryland Censor									from 19 Aug √	last known 3 Feb √
[Baltimore] Mechanics' Gazette						from 14 Mar; last known 13 Sept √				
[Baltimore] Morning Chronicle										from 8 Apr √
[Baltimore] National Museum				(prospectus issue 27 Aug) from 13 Nov √	last known 12 Mar √					
Baltimore Patriot			from 28 Dec	√	√	√		√	√	√
[Baltimore] People's Advocate							only known 24 Apr (imperfect)			
[Baltimore] People's Friend							from 25 May; last known 27 Sept √			
Baltimore Price-Current	√	√	√	√	√	√	√	√	√	√
Baltimore Recorder	only known 16 June									
[Baltimore] Scourge	first & last known: 2 June & 24 Nov √									
[Baltimore] Sun		from 24 June √	√	last known 7 Jan ×		√	last known 9 Feb ×			
Baltimore Telegraph					first known 9 June ×					

MARYLAND continued	1810	1811	1812	1813	1814	1815	1816	1817	1818	1819
[Baltimore] Whig	√	√	√	√	last known 6 May ×					
[Cumberland] Allegany Freeman				first known 11 Dec ×	×	○	last known 27 July ×			
[Cumberland] Alleghany Federalist							only known 6 July			
Cumberland Gazette					only known 21 July					
[Cumberland] Western Herald										first & only other known: 5 & 12 Apr √
Easton Gazette									first known 6 July ×	√
[Easton] People's Monitor	×	×	×	√	×	last known 23 Dec √				
[Easton] Republican Star	√	√	√	√	√	√	√	√	√	√
[Elizabethtown] Maryland Herald	√	√	√	√	√	√	√	√	√	√
[Fredericktown] Bartgis's Republican Gaz.	√	√	√	√	√	×	×	√	√	√
[Fredericktown] Freiheitsbothe	only known 14 Apr									
[Fredericktown] General Staatsbothe		only known 27 Dec								
Frederick-Town Herald	√	√	√	√	√	√	√	√	√	√
[Fredericktown] Hornet	√	last known before suspension 9 Oct √		resumed 21 July √	to 6 July √					
[Fredericktown] Plain Dealer				first known 29 July ×	last known 26 Oct ×					
[Fredericktown] Political Examiner				from 9 Aug √	√	×	×	√		
[Fredericktown] Star of Federalism								first known 5 Apr ×	√	√
Hagers-Town Gazette	√	√	√	last known 15 June √						
[Hagerstown] Torch Light										first known 15 June ×
[Hagerstown] Wacht-Thurm						only known 21 Apr				
[Hagerstown] Westliche Correspondenz	○	○	○	×	○	○	○	○	○	○
[Havre-de-Grace] Bond of Union									first known 23 Apr × (suspension)	(suspension) last known 21 Jan ×
Rockville Courier										only known 27 Sept ○

Page 85 SYMBOLS: √ complete or extensive coverage exists × few numbers known (usually less than 25% of those issued) ○ no copies extant   Table for 1810–1819

Chronological Tables of American Newspapers 1690–1820

Table for 1810–1819

	1810	1811	1812	1813	1814	1815	1816	1817	1818	1819
MARYLAND continued										
[Uniontown] Engine of Liberty					✓	last known 15 June ✓				
MASSACHUSETTS										
[Boston] Auction Advertiser							only known 11 Oct			
[Boston] Christian Watchman										from 29 May ✓
[Boston] Columbian Centinel	✓	✓	✓	✓	✓	✓	✓	✓	✓	✓
[Boston] Compass									from 6 June ✓ (irregular)	last known 21 Aug ✓ (irregular)
Boston Daily Advertiser				from 3 Mar ✓	✓	✓	✓	✓	✓	✓
[Boston] Evening Gazette					from 20 Aug ✓	✓	to 10 Aug ✓			
[Boston] Fredonian	from 20 Feb to 15 May ✓									
Boston Gazette	✓	✓	✓	✓	✓	✓	✓	✓	✓	✓
[Boston] Idiot								(preliminary issue 20 Dec)	from 10 Jan ✓	to 2 Jan
[Boston] Independent Chronicle	✓	✓	✓	✓	✓	✓	✓	✓	✓	✓
Boston Intelligencer							from 17 Aug ✓	✓	✓	✓
[Boston] Kaleidoscope									first known 12 Dec ✓	last known 13 Nov ✓
Boston Mirror	to 21 July ✓									
[Boston] New-England Galaxy								from 10 Oct ✓	✓	✓
[Boston] New-England Palladium	✓	✓	✓	✓	✓	✓	✓	✓	✓	✓
Boston Patriot	✓	✓	✓	✓	✓	✓	✓	✓	✓	✓
[Boston] Pilot			from 25 Sept ✓	to 16 Jan ✓						
Boston Recorder							from 3 Jan ✓	✓	✓	✓
[Boston] Repertory	✓	✓	✓	✓	✓	✓	✓	✓	✓	✓
[Boston] Satirist			from 16 Jan to 9 May ✓ (irregular)							
[Boston] Scourge		from 10 Aug to 28 Dec ✓								

MASSACHUSETTS continued	1810	1811	1812	1813	1814	1815	1816	1817	1818	1819
Boston Spectator					from 1 Jan √	to 25 Feb √				
[Boston] Weekly Messenger		from 25 Oct √	√	√	√	√	√	√	√	√
Boston Weekly Report										from 1 May √
[Boston] Yankee			from 3 Jan √	√	√	√	√	√	√	√
[Charlestown] Franklin Monitor										from 2 Jan √
[Concord] Middlesex Gazette							from 20 Apr ×	√	√	√
Dedham Gazette				from 20 Aug √	√	√	√	√	√	to 25 June √
[Fairhaven] Bristol Gazette			first known 31 July √	to 10 July √						
[Greenfield] Franklin Federalist								from 24 May to 29 Dec √		
[Greenfield] Franklin Herald			from 7 Jan √	√	√	√	√	√	√	
[Greenfield] Franklin Intelligencer									from 12 Jan; last known 23 Mar √	
Greenfield Gazette	√	to 5 Feb √								
[Greenfield] Traveller		from 12 Feb to 31 Dec √								
[Haverhill] Essex Patriot								from 10 May √	√	√
[Haverhill] Merrimack Intelligencer		√	√	√	√	√	√	to 8 Feb √		
[Leominster] Political Recorder	first & last known: 15 Mar. & 5 July ×									
Nantucket Gazette							from 6 May √	to 8 Mar √		
Nantucket Weekly Magazine								from 28 June √	to 3 Jan	
New-Bedford Gazette		from 18 Oct √	last known 17 July √							
New-Bedford Mercury	√	√	√	√	√	√	√	√	√	√
[New Bedford] Old Colony Gazette	√	to 11 Oct √								
Newburyport Herald	√	√	√	√	√	√	√	√	√	√
[Newburyport] Independent Whig	first known 5 Apr √	(suspension) last known 2 May √								

SYMBOLS: √ complete or extensive coverage exists   × few numbers known (usually less than 25% of those issued)   o no copies extant   Table for 1810–1819

Chronological Tables of American Newspapers 1690–1820

Table for 1810–1819

MASSACHUSETTS continued	1810	1811	1812	1813	1814	1815	1816	1817	1818	1819
[Northampton] Anti-Monarchist	last known 14 Nov √									
[Northampton] Democrat		from 12 Mar √	√	last known 17 Aug √						
[Northampton] Hampshire Gazette	√	√	√	√	√	√	√	√	√	√
[Northampton] Hampshire Register								only known 23 Apr		
[Pittsfield] Berkshire Reporter	√	√	×	√	√	last known 16 Nov ×				
[Pittsfield] Sun	√	√	√	√	√	√	√	√	√	√
[Salem] Essex Register	√	√	√	√	√	√	√	√	√	√
Salem Gazette	√	√	√	√	√	√	√	√	√	√
[Springfield] Hampden Federalist			first known 6 Aug √	√	√	√	√	√	√	√
[Springfield] Hampden Patriot									from 31 Dec	√
[Springfield] Hampshire Federalist	√	√	to 23 July √							
[Stockbridge] Berkshire Herald					first known 22 Dec √	to 23 Nov √				
[Stockbridge] Berkshire Star						from 30 Nov √	√	√	√	√
[Stockbridge] Farmer's Herald	×	√	√	√	last known 24 Nov √					
[Worcester] Massachusetts Spy	√	√	√	√	√	√	√	√	√	√
[Worcester] National Aegis	√	√	√	√	√	√	√	√	√	√
MICHIGAN										
Detroit Gazette								from 25 July √	√	√
MISSISSIPPI										
Natchez Gazette		from 20 June √		last known 28 July ×						
[Natchez] Independent Press										from 24 Mar; last known 19 May √
[Natchez] Mississippi Republican			first known 29 Apr ×	×	√	×	○	×	√	√
[Natchez] Mississippi State Gazette									from 3 Jan √	suspended 4 Sept; resumed 4 Dec √

MISSISSIPPI continued	1810	1811	1812	1813	1814	1815	1816	1817	1818	1819
[Natchez] Mississippian	last known 10 Sept ×									
[Natchez] Washington Republican						from 17 Nov √	√	to 27 Dec √		
[Natchez] Weekly Chronicle	√	last known 8 Apr √								
Port-Gibson Correspondent										first known 27 Mar
Washington Republican				from 13 Apr √	√	to 11 Nov √				
MISSOURI										
[Franklin] Missouri Intelligencer										from 23 Apr √
[Jackson] Missouri Herald										first known 13 Aug √
St. Louis Enquirer										first known 17 Mar √
[St. Louis] Missouri Gazette	√	√	√	√	√	√	√	√	√	√
NEW HAMPSHIRE										
[Amherst] Farmer's Cabinet	√	√	√	√	√	√	√	√	√	√
Concord Gazette	√	√	√	√	√	√	√	√	√	last known 1 May √
[Concord] New-Hampshire Patriot	√	√	√	√	√	√	√	√	√	
Concord Observer										from 4 Jan √
[Dover] Strafford Register									from 25 Aug √	√
[Dover] Sun	√	(suspension) ×	×	√	√	√	√	√	to 18 Aug √	
[Exeter] Constitutionalist		suspended 4 June √	resumed 23 June √	√	to 14 June √					
[Exeter] Watchman							from 1 Oct √	√	√	√
[Hanover] American							from 7 Feb √	last known 2 Apr √		
[Hanover] Dartmouth Gazette	√	suspended 24 Apr; resumed 5 June √	√	√	√	√	√	√	√	√
[Haverhill] Advertiser	first & last known: 7 June & 19 July √									
[Haverhill] Coos Courier	last known 15 Mar √									

Page 89   SYMBOLS: √ complete or extensive coverage exists   × few numbers known (usually less than 25% of those issued)   o no copies extant   Table for 1810–1819

Chronological Tables of American Newspapers 1690–1820

Table for 1810–1819

	1810	1811	1812	1813	1814	1815	1816	1817	1818	1819
NEW HAMPSHIRE continued										
[Keene] New Hampshire Sentinel	✓	✓	✓	✓	✓	✓	✓	✓	✓	✓
[Portsmouth] Herald of Gospel Liberty	suspended at Portsmouth 13 Apr ✓				resumed 4 Feb; suspended 9 Dec ✓	resumed 3 Feb; susp. 29 Sept; except 22 Dec ✓	8 Mar (extra)			
[Portsmouth] Intelligencer	✗	✗	✗	✓	✓	✓	✓	to 15 May ✓		
[Portsmouth] New-Hampshire Gazette	✓	✓	✓	✓	✓	✓	✓	✓	✓	✓
Portsmouth Oracle	✓	✓	✓	✓	✓	✓	✓	✓	✓	✓
[Portsmouth] Oracle of New-Hampshire								from 22 May; last known 11 Sept ✓		
[Portsmouth] People's Advocate							from 24 Sept ✓	to 17 May ✓		
[Portsmouth] War Journal				from 12 Mar to 10 Dec ✓						
[Walpole] Democratic Republican			from 4 July ✓	to 5 July ✓						
[Walpole] Farmer's Weekly Museum	to 15 Oct ✓									
NEW JERSEY										
[Bridgeton] East-Jersey Republican							first & last known: 22 May. & 3 July ✓			
[Bridgeton] Washington Whig						from 24 July ✓	✓	✓	✓	✓
[Burlington] Rural Visiter	from 30 July ✓	to 22 July ✓								
[Camden] Gloucester Farmer										first & last known: 7 Jan & 2 Nov ✗
[Elizabeth Town] Essex Patriot			from 1 Dec ✗	last known 21 Dec ✗						
Elizabeth-Town Gazette									from 8 Sept ✓	✓
[Elizabeth Town] New-Jersey Journal	✓	✓	✓	✓	✓	✓	✓	✓	✓	✓
[Freehold] Monmouth Star					first known 20 June ✗	last known 20 Feb ✗				
[Freehold] Spirit of Washington		last known 5 Mar ✗								
[Morristown] Genius of Liberty	✗		first known 7 Jan ✗	✗	last known 14 Apr ✗					
Morris-Town Herald							only known 21 Mar			
[Morristown] Memorandum										

NEW JERSEY continued	1810	1811	1812	1813	1814	1815	1816	1817	1818	1819
[Morristown] Palladium of Liberty	√	√	√	√	√	√	×	√	√	√
Mount-Holly Advertiser							only known 11 Jan			
[Mount Holly] Burlington Mirror									from 16 Sept √	to 8 Sept √
[Mount Holly] New-Jersey Mirror										from 15 Sept √
[Mount Holly] Spirit of Washington						only known 25 Mar √				
[New Brunswick] Fredonian		first known 24 Apr √	√	√	√	√	√	√	√	√
[New Brunswick] Guardian	×	√	√	√	×	×	last known 22 Feb ×			
[New Brunswick] Republican Herald	first & only other known: 7 & 14 Feb									
[New Brunswick] Times						from 1 June √				
[Newark] Centinel of Freedom	√	√	√	√	√	√	√	√	√	√
Newark Messenger								from 10 Oct √	last known 20 Nov √	
Newark Patriot										from 1 Jan; last known 2 Apr √
[Newton] Sussex Register				first known 7 Sept √	√	√	√	√	√	√
[Paterson] Bee							first & last known: 23 Jan & 2 July ×			
[Paterson] Bergen Express									first known 29 Apr ×	last known 25 Aug ×
[Perth Amboy] New-Jersey Gazette										from 4 Feb √
Salem Messenger										from 18 Sept √
[Salem] West-Jersey Gazette								first known 20 Aug ×	×	last known 13 Jan ×
[Trenton] Federalist	√	√	√	√	√	√	√	√	√	√
[Trenton] True American	√	√	√	√	√	√	√	√	√	√
[Woodbury] Columbian Herald								from 1 Jan; last known 26 Feb √		
[Woodbury] Gloucester Farmer										from 23 Sept √

SYMBOLS: √ complete or extensive coverage exists   × few numbers known (usually less than 25 % of those issued)   o no copies extant   Table for 1810–1819

Chronological Tables of American Newspapers 1690–1820

NEW YORK	1810	1811	1812	1813	1814	1815	1816	1817	1818	1819
Albany Advertiser						first known 30 Sept √	√	to 22 Mar √	√	√
Albany Argus				from 26 Jan √	√	√	√	√	√	√
[Albany] Balance	√	to 24 Dec √								
Albany Daily Advertiser						from 25 Sept √	√	to 24 Mar √		
Albany Gazette	×	√	√	√	√	√	×	√	√	√
[Albany] Geographical & Military Museum					from 28 Feb; last known 6 June √					
[Albany] Plough Boy										from 5 June √
Albany Register	√	√	√	√	√	√	√	suspended 13 May; resumed 4 July √	×	√
Albany Republican			from 11 Apr to 21 July √							
[Auburn] Advocate of the People							from 18 Sept √	√	to 11 Mar √	
[Auburn] Castigator										first known 23 June ×
[Auburn] Cayuga Patriot					first known 26 Oct √	×	×	×	×	×
[Auburn] Cayuga Republican										from 24 Mar √
[Auburn] Cayuga Tocsin				first known 2 June √	last known 13 July √					
Auburn Gazette							from 12 June √	√	√	to 17 Mar √
[Auburn] Western Federalist	first known 17 Jan ×	√	√	√	o	o	last known 10 Jan ×			
[Ballston Spa] Independent American	√	√	√	√	√	√	√	√	to 6 May √	
[Ballston Spa] People's Watch-Tower									from 13 May ×	×
[Ballston Spa] Rural Visiter			first & only other known: 5 May & 23 June.							
[Ballston Spa] Saratoga Advertiser	√	√	to 31 Mar √							
[Ballston Spa] Saratoga Courier						first known 6 Dec √	×	last known 18 June ×		
[Ballston Spa] Saratoga Journal					first known 1 Feb √	×	×	×	to 11 Feb ×	
[Ballston Spa] Saratoga Patriot			from 19 Aug √	last known 28 Dec √						

NEW YORK continued	1810	1811	1812	1813	1814	1815	1816	1817	1818	1819
[Ballston Spa] Saratoga Republican									first known 8 Apr x	x
[Batavia] Cornucopia	last known 2 Feb √									
[Batavia] Republican Advocate		first known 16 Nov x	x	x	x	x	x	o	o	o
[Batavia] Spirit of the Times										first known 30 July x
[Bath] Farmers Gazette								only known 22 July		
[Bath] Steuben Patriot							from 26 Nov √	x	o	o
[Bath] Western Republican										first known 15 Dec √
[Binghamton] Broome County Patriot			from 10 Nov √	to 18 May √						
[Binghamton] Phoenix					first known 14 Dec x	x	o	last known 23 Sept x		
[Binghamton] Political Olio				from 25 May x	last known 5 Apr x					
[Brooklyn] Long Island Star	√	√	√	√	√	√	√	√	√	√
Buffalo Gazette		from 3 Oct √	√	√	√	√	√	√	to 14 Apr √	√
[Buffalo] Niagara Journal						from 4 July √	x	x	x	√
[Buffalo] Niagara Patriot									from 21 Apr √	√
[Caldwell] Lake George Watchman									first known 2 Oct x	x
[Canandaigua] Genesee Messenger	last known 16 Oct √									
[Canandaigua] Ontario Messenger	from 4 Dec √	x	√	√	√	√	x	x	x	√
[Canandaigua] Ontario Repository	√	√	√	√	√	√	√	√	√	√
[Catskill] American Eagle	√	last known 8 May x								
[Catskill] Greene & Del. Washingtonian							only known 31 July			
Catskill Recorder	√	√	√	x	√	√	√	√	√	√
[Cazenovia] Pilot	√	√	√	√	√	√	√	√	√	√
Cherry-Valley Gazette									from 8 Oct √	√

Page 93   SYMBOLS: √ complete or extensive coverage exists   x few numbers known (usually less than 25% of those issued)   o no copies extant   Table for 1810–1819

Chronological Tables of American Newspapers 1690–1820

Table for 1810–1819

NEW YORK continued	1810	1811	1812	1813	1814	1815	1816	1817	1818	1819
[Cherry Valley] Otsego Republican Press			from 14 Aug √	to 6 Aug √						
Cooperstown Federalist	√	√	√	×	×	×	last known 18 Apr ×			
[Cooperstown] Freeman's Journal									first known 30 Nov ×	√
[Cooperstown] Otsego Herald	√	√	√	√	√	√	√	√	√	√
[Cooperstown] Watch-Tower					first known 18 May ×	×	×	×	o	×
Cortland Republican						from 30 June √	√	√	√	√
[Delhi] Delaware Gazette										from 18 Nov √
[Elizabethtown] Essex Patriot								only known 10 June		
[Elizabethtown] Reveille			from 22 Apr √	o	last known 16 Nov ×					
[Fredonia] Chautauque Gazette								first known 11 Mar ×	×	×
Geneva Gazette	√	√	√	√	√	√	√	√	√	√
Geneva Palladium							from 10 Jan ×	×	×	×
[Glen's Falls] Adviser						from 10 Mar; only other known 14 Apr				
[Glenn's Falls] Warren Republican				first & last known: 24 June & 23 Sept ×						
[Goshen] Independent Republican							first known 16 Dec ×	×	×	×
[Goshen] Orange County Gazette	×	×	o	×	×	o	×	o	last known 18 Aug ×	
[Goshen] Orange County Patriot	√	√	√	√	√	√	√	√	√	√
Hamilton Gazette							only known 23 May			
Hamilton Recorder	from 4 Jan √									from 11 June ×
[Herkimer] American	last known 2 Aug √	√	×	×	×	×	×	o	×	o
[Herkimer] Bunker-Hill		first known 12 Sept √	last known 17 Sept √							
[Herkimer] Honest American		last known 23 May ×								
Herkimer Intelligencer	first known 22 Nov ×									

NEW YORK continued	1810	1811	1812	1813	1814	1815	1816	1817	1818	1819
[Homer] Cortland Courier		first known 26 June ×	last known 22 July ×							
[Homer] Cortland Repository				first known 15 Dec ×	×	o	o	o	×	(suspension?) o
[Homer] Farmers' Journal			first known 11 Nov ×	last known 13 Jan ×						
[Hudson] Bee	✓	✓	✓	×	✓	✓	✓	✓	×	✓
[Hudson] Northern Whig	✓	✓	✓	✓	✓	✓	✓	✓	✓	✓
[Ithaca] American Journal								from 20 Aug ×	o	✓
Ithaca Gazette								only known 5 June		
[Ithaca] Seneca Republican						only known 21 Oct				
[Johnstown] Montgomery Monitor	×	✓	×	×	×	×	×	×	o	o
[Johnstown] Montgomery Republican	×	o	×	×	×	×	×	o	o	o
[Kingston] Plebeian	✓	✓	✓	✓	✓	to 25 July ✓				
[Kingston] Ulster Gazette	×	×	×	×	×	×	o	×	×	×
[Kingston] Ulster Plebeian						from 1 Aug ✓	✓	✓	✓	×
Lansingburgh Gazette	✓	✓	✓	✓	✓	✓	×	×	o	×
[Manlius] Onondaga Herald										only known 24 Feb
Manlius Times	×	×	×	×	×	o	×	o	last known 23 Sept ×	
[Mayville] Chautauque Eagle										from 15 May ✓
[Montgomery] Independent Republican				from 26 Jan ✓	×	×	last known 8 Oct ×			
[Morrisville] Madison County Gazette									first known 23 Apr ×	×
[Moscow] Genesee Farmer								first known 27 Mar ×	×	o
[Mount Pleasant] Westchester Herald									from 15 Jan ✓	✓
New-York Advertiser								from 26 Mar ✓	✓	✓
[New York] American										from 3 Mar ✓

SYMBOLS: ✓ complete or extensive coverage exists   × few numbers known (usually less than 25% of those issued)   o no copies extant   Table for 1810–1819

Chronological Tables of American Newspapers 1690–1820

Table for 1810–1819

NEW YORK continued	1810	1811	1812	1813	1814	1815	1816	1817	1818	1819
[New York] American Citizen	to 19 Nov √									
[New York] Booksellers' Advertiser				only known May						
[New York] Booksellers' Reporter						only known Oct				
[New York] Columbian	√	√	√	√	√	√	√	√	√	√
[New York] Columbian Herald								only known 15 Feb		
[New York] Commercial Advertiser	√	√	√	√	√	√	√	√	√	√
[New York] Courier						from 9 Jan √	√	to 8 Apr √		
New-York Daily Advertiser								from 9 Apr √	√	√
[New York] Daily Express				first & last known: 3 Sept & 15 Dec ×						
[New York] Daily Items						first known 15 Nov ×	(suspension) last known 16 Feb √			
[New York] Daily Telegraph				first & only other known: 19 Feb & 13 Apr.						
New-York Evening Post	√	√	√	√	√	√	√	√	√	√
[New York] Exile								from 4 Jan; last known 18 Oct √		
New-York Gazette	√	√	√	√	√	√	√	√	√	√
[New York] Harmer's New York Register				only known 24 Mar						
New-York Herald	√	√	√	√	√	√	√	to 15 Nov √		
[New York] Independent Mechanic		from 6 Apr √	last known 26 Sept √							
New York Journal	√	last known 7 Aug √								
[New York] Ladies' Weekly Museum								from 3 May to 25 Oct √		
[New York] Mercantile Advertiser	√	√	√	√	√	√	×	×	√	√
New-York Messenger					first & only other known: 25 Nov & 6 Dec					first of two issues known 14 Dec
[New York] Mid-day Courier										
[New York] Military Monitor			from 17 Aug √	(suspension) last known 6 Nov √						

NEW YORK continued

	1810	1811	1812	1813	1814	1815	1816	1817	1818	1819
New-York Morning Post	from 20 Nov √	√	to 19 Aug √							
[New York] Morning Star	first known 4 Dec ×	√	last known 15 Dec ×							
[New York] National Advocate			from 15 Dec √	√	√	√	√	√	√	√
[New York] Observer	resumed 14 Oct √	last known 21 Apr √								
[New York] Olio				from 27 Jan √	suspended 22 Jan; other known 5 Feb √					
New-York Patriot						first known 9 Dec ×	last known 30 Mar √			
New-York Phoenix			first & last known: 12 Aug & 15 Oct √							
[New York] Political Bulletin	from 22 Dec √	last known 30 Mar √								
New-York Price-Current	√	√	√	√	√	√	√	√	last known 10 Jan ×	
[New York] Public Advertiser	√	√	√	to 22 Feb √						
New-York Public Sale Report						first known 30 Jan √	√	√	last known 14 Mar ×	
[New York] Republican Chronicle								from 2 Apr √	√	last known 27 Jan √
[New York] Republican Watch-Tower	to 16 Nov √									
[New York] Shamrock	from 15 Dec √	√	√	suspended 5 June √	resumed 18 June √	suspended 28 Jan; resumed 2 Sept √	suspended 17 Aug; resumed 2 Dec √	last known 16 Aug √		
New-York Shipping and Commercial List						from 21 Feb √	√	√	√	√
[New York] Spectator	√	√	√	√	√	√	√	√	√	√
[New York] Standard of Union				from 5 Oct √	last known 6 May √					
[New York] Star in the West			from 20 Aug √	to 23 Aug √						
[New York] Statesman										from 6 Mar; last known 23 Dec √
[New York] Times				only known 16 Nov						
[New York] United States' Shipping List		first known 22 Nov √	last known 20 Nov ×							
[New York] War			from 27 June √	√	suspended 6 Sept √			revived for three issues in Feb √		
[New York] Washington Republican	last known 13 Jan ×									

Page 97   SYMBOLS: √ complete or extensive coverage exists   × few numbers known (usually less than 25% of those issued)   o no copies extant   Table for 1810–1819

Chronological Tables of American Newspapers 1690–1820

Table for 1810–1819

NEW YORK continued	1810	1811	1812	1813	1814	1815	1816	1817	1818	1819
New York Weekly Messenger			first known 27 June ×	last known 2 Oct ×						
New-York Weekly Museum	✓	✓	✓	✓	✓	✓	✓	to 26 Apr ✓		
New York Weekly Observer		only known 29 Sept								
[New York] Weekly Visitor								from 1 Nov ✓	✓	✓
[New York] Western Star			from 16 May ✓	to 1 May ✓						
[Newburgh] Orange County Gazette										first & last known: 22 Mar & 22 Nov ×
[Newburgh] Political Index	✓	✓	✓	✓	✓	×	✓	✓	✓	✓
Newburgh Republican		first & last known: 5 Feb & 12 Mar ✓								
[Newtown] Telegraph								first known 25 Mar ×	o	last known 5 Aug ×
[Newtown] Vedette									first known 15 Aug ×	last known 2 Oct ×
[Norwich] Chenango Weekly Advertiser		from 25 Jan ✓	last known 25 June ✓							
[Norwich] Columbian Telegraph			only known 9 Dec							
Norwich Journal							from 14 Nov ✓	✓	(suspension in Dec) ✓	resumed 9 Jan ✓
[Norwich] Republican Agriculturalist									from 10 Dec ✓	✓
[Norwich] Telegraph					only known 18 Jan					
[Norwich] Volunteer					from 4 Oct		only other known 7 Feb			
Ogdensburgh Palladium	from 27 Nov ×	×	×	last known 3 Feb ×						
[Ogdensburgh] St. Lawrence Gazette								first known 16 Dec ✓	✓	
[Onondaga] Gazette							first known 24 Apr ×	×	o	o
Onondaga Register					from 28 Sept ✓	✓	✓	✓	✓	✓
Oswego Palladium										first known 14 Oct ✓
[Ovid] Seneca Patriot						from 25 Aug; last known 13 Oct ✓				
[Owego] American Farmer	✓	✓	last known 19 Feb ✓							

NEW YORK continued	1810	1811	1812	1813	1814	1815	1816	1817	1818	1819
Owego Gazette					first known 14 Dec ×	o	×	o	o	×
[Oxford] Chenango Patriot	first & only other known: 7 Aug & 11 Sept.									
Oxford Gazette				from 7 Dec √	√	o	×	√	o	√
Palmyra Register								from 26 Nov √	√	√
[Peekskill] Westchester Gazette	first known 28 Aug ×	×	×	o	×	o	×	o	×	o
Penn-Yan Herald			last known 6 May ×							first known 2 Mar √
[Peterboro] Freeholder	×	×								
[Plattsburgh] American Monitor	to 10 Nov √									
[Plattsburgh] Clinton Advertiser	from 17 Nov	only other known 12 Jan								
[Plattsburgh] Northern Herald			first known 11 Jan (suspension in Aug) ×	(resumption in Apr) ×	×	last known 21 July ×				
[Plattsburgh] Political Observatory		first & last known: 12 Apr. & 24 Aug √								
[Plattsburgh] Republican		from 12 Apr √	√	√	√	√	√	√	√	√
Potsdam Gazette							first known 21 June ×	×	×	×
[Poughkeepsie] Dutchess Observer						from 10 May √	√	√	√	√
Poughkeepsie Journal	√	√	√	√	√	√	√	√	√	√
[Poughkeepsie] Northern Politician			from 16 Sept to 9 Dec √							
[Poughkeepsie] Political Barometer	√	to 21 Aug √								
[Poughkeepsie] Republican Herald		from 28 Aug √	suspended 12 Sept; resumed 16 Dec √	√	√	√	√	√	o	√
Rochester Gazette									first known 9 June ×	(suspension in Dec) ×
Rochester Telegraph									from 7 July √	√
[Rome] Oneida Observer										only known 20 July
Sacket's Harbor Gazette								first known 25 Mar √	√	√
[Sag Harbor] American Eagle								first known 25 Oct √	×	√

Page 99   SYMBOLS: √ complete or extensive coverage exists   × few numbers known (usually less than 25% of those issued)   o no copies extant   Table for 1810–1819

Chronological Tables of American Newspapers 1690–1820

Table for 1810–1819

NEW YORK continued	1810	1811	1812	1813	1814	1815	1816	1817	1818	1819
[Sag Harbor] Suffolk County Recorder							from 19 Oct ✓	to 11 Oct ✓		
[Sag Harbor] Suffolk Gazette	✓	to 23 Feb ✓								
[Salem] Northern Post	✓	✓	✓	✓	✓	✓	✓	✓	✓	✓
[Salem] Washington Register	✓	✓	○	○	✓	✓	✓	✓	✓	✓
[Sandy Hill] Times										first known 9 Apr ×
[Sangerfield] Civil & Religious Intelligencer							from 18 Nov ✓	✓	×	✓
[Saratoga Springs] Saratoga Sentinel										from 26 May ✓
[Schenectady] Cabinet	first known 24 July ×	×	✓	✓	✓	×	✓	✓	✓	✓
Schenectady Gazette			from 9 July; last known 20 Aug ✓							
[Schenectady] Mohawk Advertiser	×	last known 12 Nov ×								
[Schenectady] Western Budget	last known 8 May ✓	last known 26 Oct ×								
[Schoharie] American Herald	last known 24 July ×									
Schoharie Budget								only known 18 June		
[Schoharie] Observer									first known 25 Nov ×	×
[Schoharie] True American	first known 20 Jan ×	○	○	○	○	last known 25 Feb ×				
[Sherburne] Republican Messenger	from 22 May ✓	to 1 Jan								
Somers Museum	last known 24 July ×									
[Troy] Farmers' Register	✓	✓	✓	×	✓	×	×	×	×	×
Troy Gazette	✓	×	last known 17 Mar ×							
[Troy] Northern Budget	suspended 13 Mar; resumed 19 June ✓	✓	✓	×	×	×	×	✓	✓	✓
Troy Post			from 1 Sept ✓	✓	✓	✓	✓	✓	✓	✓
[Union Springs] Cayuga Tocsin			from 2 Jan ×	last known 15 Apr ×						
Utica Club					from 11 Aug ✓	(suspension) last known 12 June ×				
[Utica] Columbian Gazette	✓	✓	✓	✓	✓	✓	✓	✓	✓	✓

NEW YORK continued	1810	1811	1812	1813	1814	1815	1816	1817	1818	1819
Utica Observer								first known 1 July ×	o	o
[Utica] Patriot	√	√	√	√	√	√	√	√	√	√
[Utica] Patrol						from 5 Jan √	to 1 Jan			
Waterford Gazette	×	×	×	×	o	o	last known 20 Feb ×			
Waterloo Gazette								first known 2 July √	√	√
[Watertown] American Advocate					only known 23 Nov					
[Watertown] American Eagle	from 10 Apr; last known 25 Sept √									
[Watertown] Hemisphere	only known 6 Feb									
[Watertown] Independent Republican										first known 14 June ×
[Watertown] Northern Luminary				first known 2 Feb ×	last known 2 Mar ×					
[Watertown] Republican Watchman			first & only other kn.: 12 May & 30 June							
[West Farms] West-Chester Patriot				only known 3 July						
NORTH CAROLINA										
Edenton Gazette	√	√	√	(suspension) √	×	o	×	×	×	√
[Fayetteville] American					first known 13 Oct ×	o	×	×	last known 23 July ×	
[Fayetteville] Carolina Observer							first known 22 Aug ×	×	×	×
Fayetteville Intelligencer		only known 22 Mar								
[Fayetteville] People's Friend						only known 15 Dec				
Halifax Compiler								first known 17 July ×	o	
[Halifax] North-Carolina Journal	last known 17 Dec ×									
Milton Intelligencer										only known 4 June
[Murfreesborough] Hornets' Nest			first known 1 Oct √	last known 4 Nov ×						
[New Bern] Carolina Centinel									from 21 Mar √	√

Page 101 SYMBOLS: √ complete or extensive coverage exists × few numbers known (usually less than 25% of those issued) o no copies extant   Table for 1810–1819

Chronological Tables of American Newspapers 1690–1820

Table for 1810–1819

NORTH CAROLINA continued	1810	1811	1812	1813	1814	1815	1816	1817	1818	1819
[New Bern] Carolina Federal Republican	×	×	✓	✓	○	×	✓	✓	last known 25 Apr ✓	
Newbern Herald	last known 26 Feb ✓									
[New Bern] True Republican	first known 2 Apr ✓	last known 7 Aug ✓								
[Raleigh] Minerva	✓	✓	✓	✓	✓	✓	✓	✓	✓	✓
Raleigh Register	✓	✓	✓	✓	✓	✓	✓	✓	✓	✓
[Raleigh] Star	✓	✓	✓	✓	✓	✓	✓	✓	✓	✓
[Tarboro] Political Synopsis					first known 17 Nov	only other known 5 Oct				
[Washington] American Recorder						first known 28 Apr ×	×	○	×	✓
[Wilmington] Cape-Fear Recorder							first known 20 May ✓	×	×	×
Wilmington Gazette	×	○	×	×	×	×	last known 13 Jan ×			
OHIO										
Cadiz Informant									only known 9 Jan	
[Canton] Ohio Repository						from 30 Mar ✓	✓	✓	✓	✓
[Chillicothe] Fredonian		from 19 Sept; suspended 3 Oct ✓	resumed 25 Aug ✓	✓	last known 20 July ×					
[Chillicothe] Independent Republican	✓	to 13 Sept ✓								
[Chillicothe] Scioto Gazette	✓	×	×	○	×	✓	×	○	✓	✓
[Chillicothe] Supporter	✓	✓	✓	✓	✓	✓	✓	✓	✓	✓
[Chillicothe] Weekly Recorder					from 5 July ✓	✓	✓	✓	✓	✓
[Cincinnati] Advertiser	from 13 June; last known 19 Dec ×									
Cincinnati Gazette						from 15 July; last known 2 Sept ✓				
[Cincinnati] Inquisitor									from 23 June ✓	✓
[Cincinnati] Liberty Hall	✓	✓	✓	✓	✓	✓	✓	✓	✓	✓
[Cincinnati] Literary Cadet										from 22 Nov ✓

OHIO continued — Table for 1810–1819

OHIO continued	1810	1811	1812	1813	1814	1815	1816	1817	1818	1819
[Cincinnati] Spirit of the West	resumed 1 Sept √				from 26 July √	to 29 Apr √				
[Cincinnati] Western Spy		√	√	√	√	√	√	√	√	√
[Cincinnati] Whig	last known 2 May √									
[Circleville] Fredonian		first known 16 Oct √	to 11 Aug √							
[Circleville] Olive Branch								first known 26 Oct × (suspension)	resumed 21 Jan ×	×
Cleaveland Gazette									from 31 July to 29 Sept √	
Cleaveland Herald										from 19 Oct √
Cleaveland Register									from 6 Oct √	√
[Clinton] Ohio Register				from 26 June ×	√	last known 5 Dec √				
Columbus Gazette								first known 4 Dec √	√	√
[Columbus] Ohio Monitor							first known 13 June √	×	√	√
[Columbus] Western Intelligencer					from 16 Mar √	×	×	last known 25 Sept ×		
[Dayton] Ohio Centinel	first known 10 May √	√	√	to 19 May √						
[Dayton] Ohio Republican				from 31 May √	√	√	last known 9 Oct √			
[Dayton] Ohio Watchman								first known 16 Oct √	√	√
Delaware Gazette										first known 22 July ×
[Eaton] Western Telegraph								only known 5 Dec		
[Franklinton] Freeman's Chronicle			from 24 June √	√	last known 14 Nov √					
[Gallipolis] Gallia Gazette										first known 2 Apr √
Hamilton Gazette										from 12 Oct √
[Hamilton] Miami Herald					from 22 June √	√	last known 2 Feb √			
[Hamilton] Miami Intelligencer								from 12 Sept √	√	to 5 Oct √
[Hamilton] Philanthropist							from 29 Mar √	last known 18 Apr √		

SYMBOLS: √ complete or extensive coverage exists   × few numbers known (usually less than 25% of those issued)   o no copies extant

Chronological Tables of American Newspapers 1690–1820

Table for 1810–1819

OHIO continued	1810	1811	1812	1813	1814	1815	1816	1817	1818	1819
Hillsborough Gazette									from 18 June ✓	✓
[Lancaster] Independent Press			only known 12 Sept							
[Lancaster] Ohio Eagle			first known 30 Oct ✗	✗	✗	✗	○	✓	✓	✓
[Lancaster] Political Observatory	first & only other known: 8 & 15 Sept									
[Lebanon] Farmer							from 13 Dec ✓	✓	last known 29 Aug ✓	
[Lebanon] Western Star	(suspension) ✗	✗	✗	✗	○	✗	✓	✓	✓	✓
[Marietta] American Friend				from 24 Apr ✓	suspended 26 Feb; resumed 9 Apr ✓	✓	suspended 12 Jan; resumed 15 Mar ✓	✓	suspended 6 Mar; resumed 8 May ✓	suspended 24 Dec ✓
[Marietta] Commentator	last known 26 June ✓									
[Marietta] Ohio Gazette	✗	last known 9 Dec ✗								
[Marietta] Western Spectator	first known 30 Oct ✓	✓	✓	suspended 26 May; resumed & ended 31 July ✓						
[Mount Pleasant] Philanthropist								from 29 Aug ✓	✓	✓
[Mount Vernon] Ohio Register							from 24 Apr ✓	✓	last known 15 Apr ✓	
[New Lisbon] Ohio Patriot	✗	✗	✗	✗	✗	✗	✗	✗	✓	✓
Portsmouth Gazette	○	✗		✗	○	✗	✗	✗	from 5 Aug ✓	to 17 Mar ✓
[St. Clairsville] Ohio Federalist				from 11 May ✓	✓	✓	✓	✗	last known 2 July ✗	
[Springfield] Farmer										from 13 Feb ✓
[Steubenville] Western Herald	○	✗	✗	✗	○	✓	✓	✓	✓	✓
[Urbana] Farmer's Watch-Tower			first known 28 Oct ✗	last known 11 Aug ✗						
Urbana Gazette								first known 23 Dec .	only other known 16 Sept .	
[Urbana] Spirit of Liberty							only known 16 Apr			
[Warren] Trump of Fame			from 9 June ✓	✓	✓	✓	to 27 Sept ✓			
[Warren] Western Reserve Chronicle							first known 11 Oct ✓	✓	✓	✓
[West Union] Political Censor							first known 16 July ✓	✗	✗	✗

OHIO continued	1810	1811	1812	1813	1814	1815	1816	1817	1818	1819
[Williamsburg] Political Censor					only known 30 Aug					
[Williamsburg] Western American					first known 17 Sept ×	last known 11 Mar ×				
[Wilmington] True American							only known 15 Aug			
[Wooster] Ohio Spectator								first known 21 Nov ×	o	×
[Worthington] Western Intelligencer		from 17 July √	√	√	last known 19 Jan √					
[Xenia] Ohio Vehicle					first known 2 July ×	√	last known 9 Jan ×			
Xenia Patriot							first & last known: 28 May & 19 Sept ×			
[Xenia] Reading Room										first known 6 May √
Zanesville Express	first known 6 Jan √	√	√	√	√	√	√	×	×	×
[Zanesville] Muskingum Messenger		√	√	√	√	√	√	√	√	√
PENNSYLVANIA										
[Allentown] Friedens-Bothe			from 28 Sept √	√	√	√	√	√	√	√
[Allentown] Unabhängige Republikaner	from 27 July √	√	√	√	√	√	√	√	√	√
[Beaver] Crisis				from 22 May ×	×	×	last known 27 Apr ×			
Beaver Gazette				only known 8 June						
Beaver Gazette								only known 4 Jan		
[Beavertown] Minerva	o	last known 21 Sept ×								
[Beaver-Town] Western Cabinet		from 28 Sept ×	×	last known 15 May (imperfect) ×						
Bedford Gazette	×	×	o	o	o	o	o	o	o	o
[Bedford] True American				from 2 July √	√	√	×	o	o	o
[Bellefonte] American Patriot					from 5 Feb √	√	×	last known 22 Sept √		
Bellefonte Patriot									first known 8 June √	×
[Bethany] Wayne County Mirror									first known 28 Mar ×	×

SYMBOLS: √ complete or extensive coverage exists   × few numbers known (usually less than 25% of those issued)   o no copies extant   Table for 1810–1819

PENNSYLVANIA continued	1810	1811	1812	1813	1814	1815	1816	1817	1818	1819
[Brownsville] American Telegraph					from 9 Nov √	√	√	√	to 4 Mar √	
[Brownsville] Western Register										first known 22 Mar ×
[Brownsville] Western Repository	only known 23 May									
Butler Palladium									from 20 June ×	last known 17 Apr ×
[Carlisle] American Volunteer					from 15 Sept √	√	√	√	√	√
[Carlisle] Cumberland Register	√	√	√	√	last known 22 June ×					
[Carlisle] Freyheits-Fahne					from 27 Aug √	√	√	last known 25 Mar √		
Carlisle Gazette	√	√	√	√	√	√	√	last known 23 Oct √		
Carlisle Herald	√	√	√	√	√	√	√	√	○	○
Carlisle Republican								from 10 Nov √	√	last known 27 Apr √
[Carlisle] Spirit of the Times	○	○	○	last known 27 Aug ×						
[Carlisle] Unpartheyische Americaner										from 11 May √
[Chambersburg] Democratic Republican						from 7 Nov √	√	to 12 May √		
[Chambersburg] Franklin Repository	√	√	√	×	√	√	×	√	√	√
[Chambersburg] Franklin Republican										first known 13 Apr ×
[Chambersburg] Republican	only known 26 June									
[Columbia] Columbian										
[Columbia] Susquehanna Waterman			first known 12 Mar ×	○	○	last known 13 Oct ×				
[Danville] Express							only known 26 Jan			
[Downingtown] American Republican	√	√	√	√	√	√	√	√	√	√
[Doylestown] Bucks County Messenger							first known 24 Sept √	√	√	
Doylestown Democrat										from 28 June √
[Doylestown] Pennsylvania Correspondent	√	√	√	√	√	√	√	√	√	√

PENNSYLVANIA continued	1810	1811	1812	1813	1814	1815	1816	1817	1818	1819
Easton Centinel								from 11 July ✓	✓	✓
Eastoner-Deutsche Patriot	○	×	○	×	last known 9 Mar ×					
[Easton] Northampton Correspondent	×	○	○	○	×	×	×	×	×	×
[Easton] Northampton Farmer	×	×	○	×	last known 2 Apr ×					
[Easton] Pennsylvania Herald	to 1 Aug ✓									
[Easton] People's Instructor	from 8 Aug ✓	✓	✓	to 26 May ✓						
[Easton] Spirit of Pennsylvania						from 16 June ✓	✓	○	○	○
[Edentown] Eden Star					first known 2 May ✓	last known 4 Sept ×				
[Erie] Genius of the Lakes							first known 26 Oct (suspension)			only other known 27 Mar
[Erie] Northern Centinel					first known 1 Apr ✓ (suspension)	last known 28 June ×				
Erie Patriot										only known 20 Feb
[Frankford] Spirit of '76			only known 27 Feb							
Frankford Weekly Messenger	only known 18 May									only known 23 July
[Germantown] Columbian Advocate										
[Gettysburg] Adams Centinel	✓	✓	✓	✓	✓	✓	✓	✓	✓	✓
[Gettysburg] Republican Compiler									from 16 Sept ✓	✓
Greensburgh & Indiana Register		from 9 July ✓	✓	○	○	×	last known 23 Mar ×			
[Greensburg] Farmers Register	last known 29 June ×									
Greensburgh Gazette		from 22 Aug ✓	✓	✓	✓	✓	✓	✓	✓	✓
[Greensburgh] Westmoreland & Ind. Reg.		first known 12 July ✓	to 2 July ✓							
[Greensburg] Westmoreland Republican		first known 8 Aug ×							from 25 Apr ✓	✓
Hannover Gazette			○	○	○	×	○	×	○	○
Hanover Guardian		first known 8 Aug ✓								first known 21 Apr ✓

SYMBOLS: ✓ complete or extensive coverage exists   × few numbers known (usually less than 25 % of those issued)   ○ no copies extant   Table for 1810–1819

Chronological Tables of American Newspapers 1690–1820

Table for 1810–1819

PENNSYLVANIA continued	1810	1811	1812	1813	1814	1815	1816	1817	1818	1819
[Harrisburg] Chronicle				from 31 May √	√	√	√	√	√	√
[Harrisburg] Dauphin Guardian	√	last known 12 Nov √								
Harrisburger Morgenröthe Zeitung	√	√	√	√	○	×	×	○	×	○
[Harrisburgh] Oracle of Dauphin	√	√	√	√	√	√	√	√	√	√
[Harrisburg] Pennsylvania Republican		from 3 Dec √	√	√	√	√	to 26 Nov √			
Harrisburg Republican							from 3 Dec √	√	√	√
[Harrisburg] Times	first known after suspension 19 May	last known 31 Aug ×								
[Huntingdon] American Eagle	only known 23 Aug									
Huntingdon Gazette	√	√	√	√	√	√	√	√	√	√
Huntingdon Intelligencer					first & last known: 26 May & 13 Oct ×					
Huntingdon Republican					first known 27 Oct ×	○	×	○	○	last known 15 July ×
[Indiana] American						first known 9 Feb (extra) ×	○	○	○	○
[Kittanning] Armstrong True American				only known 14 May						
[Kittanning] Western Eagle	from 20 Sept	only other known 12 July								
[Lancaster] Americanische Staatsbothe	√	○	×	×	×	×	×	×	×	×
[Lancaster] Free Press										from 10 May √
[Lancaster] Intelligencer	√	(except 9 Mar) √	√	√	√	√	√	√	√	√
Lancaster Journal	√	√	√	√	√	√	√	√	√	√
[Lancaster] Pennsylvania Farmer			from 26 Aug √	last known 1 Sept √						
[Lancaster] Pennsylvania Gazette								from 12 Aug √	√	×
[Lancaster] Times	last known 17 Mar √									
[Lancaster] Volksfreund	√	√	√	√	√	√	√	√	×	×
[Lancaster] Wahre Amerikaner	√	√	○	○	○	○	○	○	○	○

PENNSYLVANIA continued	1810	1811	1812	1813	1814	1815	1816	1817	1818	1819
[Lebanon] Libanoner Morgenstern	✓	✓	o	×	o	×	o	×	×	o
[Lebanon] Unpartheyische Berichter							first known 29 Nov ✓	×	o	×
[Lewistown] Juniata Gazette						first known 14 Apr ×	o	×	o	×
Marietta Pilot				first known 30 Nov ✓	✓	✓	✓	×	last known 3 Jan	
[Meadville] Crawford Weekly Messenger	✓	✓	✓	✓	✓	✓	✓	✓	✓	✓
[Mercer] Western Press		first known 18 Sept ✓	✓	✓	o	o	o	×	×	×
[Mifflinburg] Advocate of Union							first & only other known: 5 & 12 July			
[Mifflintown] Mifflin Eagle								first known 15 Nov ×	o	o
[Milton] Miltonian							from 21 Sept ✓	✓	✓	✓
Montrose Gazette							from 20 Feb ✓	✓	from 16 May ✓	✓
[Montrose] Susquehannah Centinel						first known 21 June ×	last known 1 Feb ×			
[Newtown] Herald of Liberty									to 9 May ✓	
[Newtown] Star of Freedom								from 21 May ✓	to 25 Mar ✓	
Norristown Herald	✓	✓	✓	✓	×	×	✓	✓	✓	✓
[Norristown] Weekly Register	✓	✓	✓	✓	✓	✓	✓	✓	✓	✓
[Northumberland] Columbia Gazette				only known 2 Nov						
[Northumberland] Republican Argus	✓	✓	last known 15 July ✓							
[Northumberland] Sunbury & N. Gazette	o	o	o	last known 29 June ×						
[Perryopolis] Comet								first & last known: 26 June & 10 July ✓		
[Philadelphia] American Centinel							from 26 Aug ×	✓	✓	✓
[Philadelphia] American Democratic Her.					from 9 May; susp. 14 May to 11 July ×	last known 4 Jan ×				
[Philadelphia] Amerikanischer Beobachter	✓									
[Philadelphia] Aurora	✓	to 29 Aug ✓	✓	✓	✓	✓	✓	✓	✓	✓

Page 109   SYMBOLS: ✓ complete or extensive coverage exists   × few numbers known (usually less than 25% of those issued)   o no copies extant   Table for 1810–1819

Chronological Tables of American Newspapers 1690–1820

Table for 1810–1819

PENNSYLVANIA continued	1810	1811	1812	1813	1814	1815	1816	1817	1818	1819
[Philadelphia] Bureau			from 28 Mar; last known 30 Dec ✓							
[Philadelphia] Corrector					only known 16 Sept					
[Philadelphia] Democratic Press	✓	✓	✓	✓	✓	✓	✓	✓	✓	✓
[Philadelphia] Evening Star	from 4 July; last known 8 Dec ✓									
[Philadelphia] Franklin Gazette									from 23 Feb ✓	✓
[Philadelphia] Freeman's Journal	✓	✓	✓	✓	✓	✓	✓	✓	✓	✓
[Philadelphia] Grotjan's Phila. P. S. Report			from 11 May ✓	✓	✓	✓	✓	✓	✓	✓
[Philadelphia] Herald of Gospel Liberty		from 5 July ✓	✓	✓	to 21 Jan ✓					
[Philadelphia] Hope's Phila. Price-Current	✓	✓	✓	last known 28 Dec ✓						
[Philadelphia] Independent Balance								first known 9 July ✓	✓	✓
[Philadelphia] Pennsylvania Democrat	suspended 4 to 26 May, to 25 Nov ✓									
[Philadelphia] Pennsylvania Gazette	✓	✓	✓	✓	✓	to 11 Oct ✓				
[Philadelphia] Political & Commercial Reg.	✓	✓	✓	✓	✓	✓	✓	✓	×	×
[Philadelphia] Poulson's Amer. Daily Adv.	✓	✓	✓	✓	✓	✓	✓	✓	✓	✓
[Philadelphia] Relfs Philadelphia Gazette	✓	✓	✓	✓	✓	✓	✓	✓		
[Philadelphia] Scott's Phila. Price-Current				from 31 May; last known 22 Nov ✓						
[Philadelphia] Spirit of the Press	○	×	×	last known Sept ×						
[Philadelphia] Star of Liberty			first & last known: 3 Nov & 25 Nov ✓							
[Philadelphia] Tickler	✓	✓	suspended 29 Apr; resumed 20 July ✓	last known 17 Nov ✓						
[Philadelphia] True American	✓	✓	✓	✓	×	✓	✓	✓	to 7 Mar ✓	
[Philadelphia] Union		✓							from 9 Mar ✓	
[Philadelphia] United States' Gazette	✓	✓	✓	✓	✓	✓	✓	✓	to 7 Mar ✓	
[Philadelphia] Voice of the Nation				first known 17 Aug ✓	last known 1 Apr ×					

PENNSYLVANIA continued	1810	1811	1812	1813	1814	1815	1816	1817	1818	1819
[Philadelphia] Wanderer				first & only other kn.:24 Mar & 21 Apr						
[Philadelphia] Whig Chronicle			from 14 Oct; last known 23 Dec √							
[Pittsburgh] Commonwealth	√	√	√	√	√	√	√	√	to 25 Apr √	√
Pittsburgh Gazette	√	√	√	√	√	√	√	√	√	√
[Pittsburgh] Mercury		from 26 Sept √	suspended 4 Apr; resumed 9 July	√	√	√	√	√	√	√
[Pittsburgh] Statesman									from 9 May √	√
Pottstown Times										from 1 July √
[Presque Isle] Mirror	√	to 1 June √								
Readinger Adler	√	√	√	√	√	√	√	√	√	√
[Reading] Berks and Schuylkill Journal							from 8 June √	√	√	√
Readinger Postbothe							from 3 Aug √	√	√	√
[Reading] Standhafte Patriot		first known 14 Aug ×		o	×	last known 25 Oct √				
[Reading] Weekly Advertiser	√	√	√	√	√	√	to 27 Apr √			
[Reading] Welt Bothe			first known 5 Feb ×	×	(suspension) √	×	×	×	×	√
[Russelville] American Star							first known 16 Sept ×	last known 8 Dec ×		
[Shippensburg] Spirit of the Times					first known 18 Sept	only other known 4 Nov				
[Shippensburg] Tree of Liberty								from 4 July to 27 Oct √		
[Somerset] Westliche Telegraph						first known 6 Apr	only other known 24 Oct			
Somerset Whig				first known 28 Oct √	√	√	√	√	√	√
[Sunbury] Nordwestliche Post									from 13 Nov √	√
[Sunbury] Northumberland Republicaner			(preliminary "Extra" 5 Aug); from 12 Aug √	√	√	√	√	√	to 2 Jan √	
Sunbury Times					first known 13 May ×	o	×	×	o	last known 27 Oct √
[Towanda] Bradford Gazette				from 10 Aug √	suspended 23 Aug √	resumed 18 Apr √	√	×	last known 13 July ×	

Page 111   SYMBOLS: √ complete or extensive coverage exists   × few numbers known (usually less than 25% of those issued)   o no copies extant   Table for 1810–1819

Chronological Tables of American Newspapers 1690–1820

Table for 1810–1819

PENNSYLVANIA continued	1810	1811	1812	1813	1814	1815	1816	1817	1818	1819
[Towanda] Mirror of the Times							only known 3 Apr			
[Towanda] Settler									from 5 Sept ×	√
[Towanda] Washingtonian							first known 14 Oct ×	last known 24 Sept √		
[Uniontown] Fayette and Greene Spectator		from 10 Jan √	last known 4 Apr ×							
[Uniontown] Genius of Liberty	×	×	×	×	×	o	o	×	√	√
Washington Examiner								from 28 May √	√	√
[Washington] Reporter	√	√	√	√	√	√	√	√	√	√
[Washington] Washingtonian			from 15 Dec ×	last known 10 Nov ×						
[Washington] Western Corrector	first known 6 Nov ×	last known 19 Feb √								
[Washington] Western Register							only known 3 Feb			
[Washington] Western Telegraphe	×	last known 18 July ×								
Waynesburgh Messenger						only known 21 Jan				
[West Chester] Chester & Del. Federalist	√	√	√	√	√	√	√	to 31 Dec √		
[Westchester] Village Record									from 7 Jan √	√
[Wilkesbarre] Advertiser		from 1 Feb √		first known 29 July √	√	last known 15 Sept √				
[Wilkesbarre] Gleaner			√	suspended 5 Mar; resumed 16 Apr √	√	√	×	×	last known 22 May ×	
[Wilkesbarre] Luzerne County Federalist	last known 28 Dec √									
[Wilkesbarre] Susquehanna Democrat	from 22 June √	√	√	√	√	√	√	√	√	√
[Wilkesbarre] Wyoming Herald									from 18 Sept √	
[Williamsport] Lycoming Advertiser					first known 10 Dec √	last known 18 Feb ×				
[Williamsport] Lycoming Gazette	×	×	×	×	×	×	o	o	o	×
[York] Expositor	first known 12 Apr ×		o	last known 3 June ×						
York Gazette						first known 27 July ×	√	√	√	√

PENNSYLVANIA continued	1810	1811	1812	1813	1814	1815	1816	1817	1818	1819
York Recorder	√	√	√	√	×	×	×	×	√	√
[York] Union's Freund						only known 17 May				
[York] Wahre Republicaner	×	o	o	×	o	×	×	o	×	×
RHODE ISLAND										
[Chepatchet] Scourge		only known 4 Dec								
Newport Mercury	√	√	√	√	√	√	√	√	√	√
[Newport] Rhode-Island Republican	√	√	√	√	√	√	√	√	√	√
Providence Centinel					from 7 Nov; last known 15 Dec √					
[Providence] Columbian Phenix	√	√	√	√	to 8 Jan √					
Providence Gazette	√	√	√	√	√	√	√	√	√	√
Providence Patriot					from 15 Jan √	√	√	√	√	√
[Providence] Rhode-Island American	√	√	√	√	√	√	√	√	√	√
[Providence] Scourge	only known 25 Aug									
[Warren] Bristol County Register	last known 7 Apr ×									
[Warren] Columbian Post-Boy			from 25 July √	last known 20 Feb √						
[Warren] Herald of the United States	×	×	last known 12 Dec √							
[Warren] Telescope				from 6 Nov √	√	√	×	last known 28 June √		
SOUTH CAROLINA										
Camden Gazette							from 4 Apr √	√	√	√
[Charleston] Carolina Gazette	√	√	√	√	√	√	√	√	√	√
[Charleston] Carolina Patriot				only known 4 Sept						
[Charleston] Carolina Weekly Messenger	last known 11 Sept ×									
[Charleston] City Gazette	√	×	√	√	√	√	√	√	√	√

Chronological Tables of American Newspapers 1690–1820

Table for 1810–1819

SOUTH CAROLINA continued	1810	1811	1812	1813	1814	1815	1816	1817	1818	1819
Charleston Courier	✓	✓	✓	✓	✓	✓	✓	✓	✓	✓
Charleston Evening Post						first known 19 Apr ×	last known 11 Sept ×			
Charleston Gazette			from 22 Aug ✓		first & last known: 1 Mar & 17 June ×					
[Charleston] Investigator				✓	last known 9 Feb ×					
[Charleston] So. Evangelical Intelligencer										from 27 Mar ✓
[Charleston] Southern Patriot					first known 3 Sept ×	✓	✓	✓	✓	✓
[Charleston] Strength of the People	last known 6 Sept ×									
[Charleston] Times	✓	✓	✓	✓	×	×	✓	✓	×	×
[Columbia] Carolina Telegraph								only known 3 Jan		
[Columbia] State Gazette	×	○	○	×	×	×	×	○	×	✓
[Columbia] Telescope						from 19 Dec ✓	✓	×	○	○
[Edgefield] Anti-Monarchist		first & last known: 9 Sept & 2 Nov ✓								
Georgetown Gazette	×	(suspension?) ○	(suspension?) ○	×	×	○	last known 21 Sept ×			
[Georgetown] Winyaw Intelligencer								first known 15 Nov ×	×	✓
[Pendleton] Miller's Weekly Messenger	✓	×	○	✓	×	○	○	○	✓	✓
TENNESSEE										
Carthage Gazette	✓	✓	×	✓	×	×	×	last known 1 July ×		
Clarksville Gazette										first known 4 Oct ×
[Clarksville] Recorder					only known 15 Dec					
[Clarksville] Tennessee Weekly Chronicle										first & last known: 27 Jan & 7 June ✓
[Clarksville] Town Gazette										from 5 July to 8 Nov ✓
[Clarksville] United States Herald	only known 11 Aug									
[Clarksville] Weekly Chronicle									first & last known: 18 Feb & 16 Sept ✓	

TENNESSEE continued	1810	1811	1812	1813	1814	1815	1816	1817	1818	1819
[Columbia] Western Chronicle	from 17 Nov ×	o	×	o	o	o	last known 1 Aug ×			
[Franklin] Advocate				only known 15 Sept (extra) ·						
[Jonesborough] East–Tennessee Patriot										first known 30 Nov ×
[Jonesborough] Manumission Intelligencer										only known 27 Apr ·
Knoxville Intelligencer										only known 14 Dec ·
Knoxville Register							from 3 Aug √	√	√	√
[Knoxville] Western Centinel	last known 8 Sept ×									
[Knoxville] Wilson's Knoxville Gazette	√	√	√	√	o	×	×	o	last known 1 Sept √	
[M'Minnville] Mountain Echo							only known 6 Jan ·			
[Nashville] Clarion	√	√	√	√	√	×	o	√	√	√
Nashville Examiner			first known 1 Sept (extra) ×	×	×	last known 27 June ×				
Nashville Gazette										from 26 May √
[Nashville] Review	√	last known 3 May ×								
Nashville Whig			first known 2 Sept √	√	√	√	√	√	√	√
Rogersville Gazette						first known 4 Nov ·			only other known 13 July ·	
[Rogersville] Western Pilot						only known 19 Aug ·				
[Shelbyville] Tennessee Herald								first known 19 Dec ×	×	×
TEXAS										
[Nacogdoches] Gaceta de Texas				only known 25 May ·						
VERMONT										
[Arlington] American Register							from 17 Dec ×	last known 9 Sept ×		
[Bellows Falls] Vermont Intelligencer								from 1 Jan √	√	√
[Bennington] Green-Mountain Farmer	√	(suspension)	√	√	√	√	to 10 June √			

Page 115   SYMBOLS: √ complete or extensive coverage exists   × few numbers known (usually less than 25% of those issued)   o no copies extant   Table for 1810–1819

Chronological Tables of American Newspapers 1690–1820

Table for 1810–1819

VERMONT continued	1810	1811	1812	1813	1814	1815	1816	1817	1818	1819
Bennington News-Letter		from 25 Mar ×				last known 14 Aug √				
[Bennington] Vermont Gazette							resumed 18 June √	√	√	√
[Brattleboro] American Yeoman								from 4 Feb √	to 27 Jan √	
[Brattleboro] Reporter	√	×	(suspension in spring) √	√	√	√	√	√	×	×
Burlington Gazette					from 9 Sept √	√	√	last known before suspension 6 Feb √		only known after suspension 28 Jan
[Burlington] Northern Intelligencer					from 5 Dec to 9 Dec √					
[Burlington] Vermont Centinel	√	√	√	√	√	√	√	√	√	√
[Danville] North Star	√	√	√	√	√	√	√	√	√	√
[Middlebury] Christian Herald							from 25 Sept to 30 Oct √			
[Middlebury] Christian Messenger							from 6 Nov √	suspended 4 June; resumed 20 Aug √	√	to 23 Nov √
[Middlebury] Columbian Patriot				from 1 Sept √	√	to 23 Aug √				
Middlebury Mercury	to 4 July √									
[Middlebury] National Standard						from 30 Aug √	√	√	√	√
[Middlebury] Vermont Mirror			from 30 Sept √	√	√	√	to 18 Sept √			
[Montpelier] Freemen's Press	√	√	last known 18 June √							
[Montpelier] Watchman	√	√	√	×	√	√	√	√	√	√
[Peacham] Green Mountain Patriot	only known after suspension 27 Jan									
[Randolph] Weekly Wanderer	last known 6 Apr √									
Rutland Herald	√	√	√	√	√	√	√	√	√	√
[Rutland] Vermont Courier	to 30 May √									
[St. Albans] Champlain Reporter	last known 28 June ×									
[St. Albans] Franklin County Advertiser	first & last known: 26 July & 29 Oct √									
[Windsor] Vermont Journal	√	√	√	√	√	√	√	√	√	√

VERMONT continued	1810	1811	1812	1813	1814	1815	1816	1817	1818	1819
[Windsor] Vermont Republican	√	√	√	√	√	√	√	√	√	√
[Windsor] Washingtonian	from 23 July √	√	√	√	√	√	to 22 Jan √			
VIRGINIA										
[Abingdon] Holston Intelligencer	only known 15 May									
[Abingdon] Political Prospect	first known 4 Jan ×	×	√	√	×	×	o	o	o	×
[Alexandria] Columbian Telescope										from 16 June √
Alexandria Gazette	√	√	√	√	suspended 23 Aug; resumed 8 Sept √	√	√	√	√	√
Alexandria Herald		from 3 June √	√	√	√	√	√	√	√	√
Danville Courier									only known 20 June	
[Danville] Roanoke Sentinel		only known 5 Feb								only known 25 Sept
[Fredericksburg] Impartial Observer										
[Fredericksburg] Virginia Herald	√	×	√	√	×	√	√	√	√	√
[Leesburg] Genius of Liberty								from 11 Jan √	√	√
[Leesburg] Washingtonian	first known 6 Feb ×	×	o	o	o	o	o	o	o	o
Lexington News-Letter										from 13 Feb √
[Lynchburg] Echo							first & last known: 6 July & 17 Aug √			
Lynchburg Press	×	o	o	×	√	√	×	√	√	√
Lynchburg Star	o	o	last known 8 Jan ×							
[Norfolk] American Beacon						from 7 Aug √	√	√	√	√
Norfolk Gazette	√	√	√	√	√	√	to 17 Sept √			
Norfolk Herald	×	√	√	√	√	√	√	√	√	(suspension in July–Aug) √
[Petersburg] American Star					first known 21 Sept √	last known 22 June √		first & last known: 30 June & 23 Dec √		
Petersburg Daily Courier										

Page 117 SYMBOLS: √ complete or extensive coverage exists × few numbers known (usually less than 25 % of those issued) o no copies extant Table for 1810–1819

Chronological Tables of American Newspapers 1690–1820

Table for 1810–1819

VIRGINIA continued	1810	1811	1812	1813	1814	1815	1816	1817	1818	1819
Petersburg Intelligencer	×	×	✓	✓	×	×	×	×	×	×
[Petersburg] Mercantile Advertiser								only known 17 Feb		
[Petersburg] Republican	×	×	×	×	×	×	○	×	✓	✓
[Richmond] American Standard		only known 20 Nov								
[Richmond] Daily Compiler				from 1 May ✓	✓	✓	✓	✓	✓	✓
[Richmond] Enquirer	✓	✓	✓	✓	✓	✓	✓	✓	✓	✓
[Richmond] Virginia Argus	✓	✓	✓	✓	✓	✓	to 19 Oct ✓			
[Richmond] Virginia Patriot	✓	✓	✓	✓	✓	✓	✓	✓	✓	✓
[Richmond] Visitor	last known 18 Aug ✓									
Staunton Eagle	(suspensions) last known 3 Oct ✓									
Staunton Observer					from 4 Aug; last known 18 Aug ✓					
[Staunton] People's Friend			from 21 Sept ✓	last known 2 Oct ✓						
[Staunton] Republican Farmer	first known 5 Dec ×	✓	✓	✓	×	○	○	○	○	○
[Staunton] Spirit of the Press		only known 18 May								
[Warrenton] Palladium of Liberty								first known 23 Aug ×	×	✓
[Winchester] Republican Constellation	from 2 Jan ×	✓	✓	✓	✓	○	×	×	✓	×
[Winchester] Virginia Centinel	×	×	×	×	○	×	×	×	×	×
[Winchester] Virginia Reformer										first & last known: 22 May ✓ & 17 July ✓
Woodstock Herald								from 24 Dec ✓	✓	✓
WEST VIRGINIA										
[Charlestown] Farmer's Repository	✓	✓	✓	✓	✓	✓	✓	✓	✓	✓
Charlestown Gazette					from 1 Apr; last known 31 Dec ×					
[Clarksburg] Bye-Stander					only known 1 Feb					

WEST VIRGINIA continued	1810	1811	1812	1813	1814	1815	1816	1817	1818	1819
[Clarksburg] Independent Virginian										from 4 Aug √
[Clarksburg] Western Virginian							only known 14 Sept			
Martinsburgh Gazette	first known 27 July √	√	√	×	√	o	o	×	o	×
[Morgantown] Monongalia Spectator							first & last known: 8 June & 20 July √			
[Shepherdstown] American Eagle							first known 25 July ×	o	×	last known 7 Jan
Wellsburgh Gazette									first known 6 Feb ×	o
[Wheeling] Va. North-Western Gazette									from 23 Apr √	√

The 'Table for 1820' begins overleaf.

Table for 1810–1819

SYMBOLS: √ complete or extensive coverage exists   × few numbers known (usually less than 25% of those issued)   o no copies extant

Chronological Tables of American Newspapers 1690–1820

	1820		
ALABAMA			
[Cahawba] Alabama Watchman	from 8 Aug √	·	+
Cahawba Press and Alabama Intelligencer	×	·	+
[Claiborne] Alabama Courier	o	·	+
[Huntsville] Alabama Republican	√	·	+
Mobile Gazette	√	·	+
[St. Stephens] Halcyon	√	·	+
ARKANSAS			
[Arkansas Post] Arkansas Gazette	√	·	+
CONNECTICUT			
[Bridgeport] Connecticut Courier	×	·	+
[Bridgeport] Republican Farmer	×	·	+
[Brooklyn] Independent Observer	first known 18 Dec ×	·	+
[Hartford] American Mercury	√	·	+
[Hartford] Connecticut Courant	√	·	+
[Hartford] Connecticut Mirror	√	·	+
[Hartford] Times	√	·	+
Litchfield Republican	√	·	+
[Middletown] Middlesex Gazette	√	·	+
[New Haven] Columbian Register	√	·	+
[New Haven] Connecticut Herald	√	·	+
[New Haven] Connecticut Journal	√	·	+
[New London] Connecticut Gazette	√	·	+
[New London] Republican Advocate	√	·	+

Table for 1820

	1820		
CONNECTICUT continued			
Norwalk Gazette	√	·	+
[Norwich] Courier	√	·	+
[Windham] Political Visitant	only known 15 May	·	
DELAWARE			
[Dover] National Recorder	first known 19 Oct √	·	+
[Wilmington] American Watchman	√	·	+
[Wilmington] Delaware Gazette	√	·	+
DISTRICT of COLUMBIA			
[Georgetown] Metropolitan	from 26 Jan √	·	+
[Georgetown] National Messenger	√	·	+
[Washington] City of Washington Gazette	√	·	+
[Washington] Daily National Intelligencer	√	·	+
[Washington] National Intelligencer	√	·	+
GEORGIA			
Athens Gazette	last known 20 Oct ×	·	+
Augusta Chronicle	√	·	+
[Augusta] Georgia Advertiser	o	·	+
Augusta Herald	√	·	+
Darien Gazette	×	·	+
[Milledgeville] Georgia Journal	√	·	+
[Milledgeville] Southern Recorder	from 15 Feb √	·	+
[Mount Zion] Missionary	first known 28 Jan ×	·	+
[Savannah] Columbian Museum	(suspension in Jan) √	·	+

GEORGIA continued	1820		
[Savannah] Georgian		√	+
Savannah Price Current	last known 18 May	x	
[Savannah] Republican		√	+
[Washington] News		o	+
ILLINOIS			
Edwardsville Spectator		√	+
[Kaskaskia] Illinois Intelligencer	to 14 Oct	√	
[Shawneetown] Illinois Gazette		√	+
[Vandalia] Illinois Intelligencer	from 14 Dec	√	+
INDIANA			
Brookville Enquirer		√	+
[Charlestown] Indiana Intelligencer	first known 27 July	x	+
[Corydon] Indiana Gazette		√	+
[Jeffersonville] Indianian		x	+
[Lawrenceburg] Indiana Oracle		√	+
[Madison] Indiana Republican		√	+
New-Albany Chronicle	first known 11 Nov	x	+
[Salem] Tocsin	first & last known: 22 Apr & 9 Sept	x	+
[Vincennes] Indiana Centinel		√	+
[Vincennes] Western Sun		√	+
KENTUCKY			
[Augusta] Bracken Sentinel		√	+
Bardstown Repository		o	+

KENTUCKY continued	1820		
[Danville] Olive Branch	first known 7 Apr	√	+
[Flemingsburg] Star	only known 29 July		+
[Frankfort] Argus of Western America		√	+
[Frankfort] Commentator		√	+
[Hopkinsville] Kentucky Republican	only known 29 July		+
[Lexington] Castigator	last known 22 Jan	x	+
[Lexington] Kentucky Gazette		√	+
Lexington Public Advertiser	from 5 Jan	√	+
[Lexington] Reporter		√	+
[Lexington] Western Monitor		√	+
[Louisville] Kentucky Herald		x	+
[Louisville] Public Advertiser		√	+
[Louisville] Western Courier		x	+
[Maysville] Eagle		o	+
[Paris] Western Citizen		√	+
[Richmond] Luminary		x	+
[Russellville] Weekly Messenger		√	+
[Shelbyville] Impartial Compiler	other of two issues known 27 May		+
[Washington] Union		o	+
LOUISIANA			
[Alexandria] Louisiana Herald		√	+
Baton-Rouge Gazette		x	+
[Jackson] Feliciana Gazette	first known 30 Dec		+

Table for 1820

SYMBOLS: √ complete or extensive coverage exists
o no copies extant
× few numbers known (usually less than 25% of those issued)
+ continued publication after 1820

Chronological Tables of American Newspapers 1690–1820

LOUISIANA continued	1820			
[New Orleans] Ami des Lois		✓	:	+
[New Orleans] Courrier de la Louisiane		✓	:	+
[New Orleans] Louisiana Advertiser	from 19 Apr	✓	:	+
[New Orleans] Louisiana Gazette		✓	:	+
[New Orleans] Orleans Gazette		✓	:	+
[St. Francisville] Asylum	first known 20 July	✗	:	+
[St. Francisville] Louisianian	last known 27 May	✓	:	+
MAINE				
Bangor Weekly Register		✗	:	+
[Bath] Maine Gazette	from 8 Dec	✓	:	+
[Belfast] Hancock Gazette	from 6 July	✓	:	+
[Brunswick] Maine Intelligencer	from 23 Sept	✓	:	+
Eastport Sentinel		✓	:	+
[Hallowell] American Advocate		✓	:	+
Hallowell Gazette		✓	:	+
[Kennebunk] Weekly Visiter		✓	:	+
[Portland] Eastern Argus		✓	:	+
[Portland] Gazette		✓	:	+
[Wiscasset] Lincoln Telegraph	from 27 Apr	✗	:	+
MARYLAND				
[Annapolis] Maryland Gazette		✓	:	+
[Annapolis] Maryland Republican		✓	:	+
[Baltimore] American		✓	:	+

Table for 1820

MARYLAND continued	1820			
[Baltimore] American Farmer		✓	:	+
[Baltimore] Federal Gazette		✓	:	+
[Baltimore] Federal Republican		✓	:	+
[Baltimore] Morning Chronicle		✓	:	+
Baltimore Patriot		✓	:	+
Baltimore Price–Current		✓	:	+
Easton Gazette		✓	:	+
[Easton] Republican Star		✓	:	+
[Elizabethtown] Maryland Herald		✓	:	+
[Fredericktown] Bartgis's Republican Gaz.		✗	:	+
Frederick–Town Herald		✓	:	+
[Fredericktown] Political Examiner		✓	:	+
[Fredericktown] Star of Federalism	last known 24 Mar	✗	:	+
[Hagerstown] Torch Light		○	:	+
[Hagerstown] Westliche Correspondenz		○	:	+
[Rockville] Centinel of Freedom	only known 14 Jan		:	+
MASSACHUSETTS				
[Boston] Agricultural Intelligencer	first known 14 Jan; to 7 July	✓	:	+
[Boston] Christian Watchman	suspended 22 Jan; resumed 12 Feb	✓	:	+
[Boston] Columbian Centinel		✓	:	+
Boston Daily Advertiser		✓	:	+
Boston Gazette		✓	:	+

MASSACHUSETTS continued — 1820

MASSACHUSETTS continued	1820		
[Boston] Independent Chronicle	√	.	+
Boston Intelligencer	√	.	+
[Boston] Ladies' Port Folio	from 1 Jan; last known 8 July √	.	
[Boston] New-England Galaxy	√	.	+
[Boston] New-England Palladium	√	.	+
Boston Patriot	√	.	+
Boston Recorder	√	.	+
[Boston] Repertory	√	.	+
[Boston] Weekly Messenger	√	.	+
Boston Weekly Report	√	.	+
[Boston] Yankee	to 20 Jan √	.	
[Charlestown] Bunker-Hill Sentinel	first & last known: 24 June & 29 July √	.	
[Charlestown] Franklin Monitor	last known 3 June √	.	
[Concord] Middlesex Gazette	√	.	+
[Dedham] Village Register	from 9 June √	.	+
[Greenfield] Franklin Herald	√	.	+
[Haverhill] Essex Patriot	√	.	+
New-Bedford Mercury	√	.	+
Newburyport Herald	√	.	+
[Northampton] Hampshire Gazette	√	.	+
[Pittsfield] Sun	√	.	+
[Salem] Essex Register	√	.	+
Salem Gazette	√	.	+

MASSACHUSETTS continued — 1820

MASSACHUSETTS continued	1820		
[Springfield] Hampden Federalist	√	.	+
[Springfield] Hampden Patriot	√	.	+
[Stockbridge] Berkshire Star	√	.	+
[Worcester] Massachusetts Spy	√	.	+
[Worcester] National Aegis	√	.	+
MICHIGAN			
Detroit Gazette	√	.	+
MISSISSIPPI			
Monticello Republican	only known 1 Apr	.	
[Natchez] Mississippi Republican	√	.	+
[Natchez] Mississippi State Gazette	√	.	+
Port-Gibson Correspondent	√	.	+
MISSOURI			
[Franklin] Missouri Intelligencer	√	.	+
[Jackson] Independent Patriot	first known 23 Dec √	.	+
[Jackson] Missouri Herald	last known 26 Aug √	.	
[St. Charles] Missourian	from 24 June √	.	+
St. Louis Enquirer	√	.	+
[St. Louis] Missouri Gazette	√	.	+
NEW HAMPSHIRE			
[Amherst] Farmer's Cabinet	√	.	+
[Amherst] Hillsboro' Telegraph	from 1 Jan √	.	+
[Concord] New-Hampshire Patriot	√	.	+

Table for 1820

SYMBOLS: √ complete or extensive coverage exists
o no copies extant

× few numbers known (usually less than 25% of those issued)
+ continued publication after 1820

NEW HAMPSHIRE continued	1820		+
Concord Observer	√	.	+
[Dover] Strafford Register	√	.	+
[Exeter] Watchman	√	.	+
[Hanover] Dartmouth Gazette	last known 23 Feb √	.	
[Hanover] Dartmouth Herald	from 21 June √	.	+
[Haverhill] Grafton & Coos Intelligencer	from 30 Nov √	.	+
[Keene] New Hampshire Sentinel	√	.	+
[Portsmouth] New-Hampshire Gazette	√	.	+
Portsmouth Oracle	√	.	+
NEW JERSEY			
[Bridgeton] Washington Whig	√	.	+
Elizabeth-Town Gazette	√	.	+
[Elizabeth Town] New-Jersey Journal	√	.	+
[Freehold] Monmouth Star	×	.	+
[Morristown] Palladium of Liberty	√	.	+
[Mount Holly] New-Jersey Mirror	√	.	+
[New Brunswick] Fredonian	√	.	+
[New Brunswick] Times	√	.	+
[Newark] Centinel of Freedom	√	.	+
[Newark] New-Jersey Eagle	from 3 Mar √	.	+
[Newton] Sussex Register	√	.	+
[Perth Amboy] New-Jersey Gazette	last known 27 July √	.	
Salem Messenger	√	.	+

NEW JERSEY continued	1820		+
[Trenton] Federalist	√	.	+
[Trenton] True American	√	.	+
[Woodbury] Columbian Herald	√	.	+
NEW YORK			
Albany Argus	√	.	+
Albany Gazette	√	.	+
[Albany] New-York Statesman	from 16 May √	.	+
[Albany] Plough Boy	√	.	+
Albany Register	suspended 12 May √	.	+
Angelica Republican	first known 14 Nov √	.	+
[Auburn] Castigator	○	.	+
[Auburn] Cayuga Patriot	√	.	+
[Auburn] Cayuga Republican	√	.	+
[Ballston Spa] People's Watch-Tower	last known 5 Apr ×	.	+
[Ballston Spa] Saratoga Republican	○	.	+
[Batavia] Republican Advocate	×	.	+
[Batavia] Spirit of the Times	×	.	+
[Bath] Steuben Patriot	○	.	+
[Bath] Western Republican	×	.	+
[Brooklyn] Long Island Star	√	.	+
[Buffalo] Niagara Journal	×	.	+
[Buffalo] Niagara Patriot	√	.	+
[Caldwell] Lake George Watchman	×	.	+

NEW YORK continued	1820		
[Canandaigua] Ontario Messenger	√	.	+
[Canandaigua] Ontario Repository	√	.	+
Catskill Recorder	√	.	+
[Cazenovia] Pilot	√	.	+
Cherry-Valley Gazette	√	.	+
[Cooperstown] Freeman's Journal	√	.	+
[Cooperstown] Otsego Herald	√	.	+
[Cooperstown] Watch-Tower	o	.	+
Cortland Republican	√	.	+
[Delhi] Delaware Gazette	√	.	+
[Fredonia] Chautauque Gazette	x	.	+
Geneva Gazette	√	.	+
Geneva Palladium	x	.	+
[Goshen] Independent Republican	√	.	+
[Goshen] Orange County Patriot	√	.	+
[Goshen] Orange Farmer	first known 12 Feb x	.	+
Hamilton Recorder	last known 13 May x	.	+
[Herkimer] American	o	.	+
[Homer] Cortland Repository	x	.	+
[Hudson] Bee	√	.	+
[Hudson] Columbia Republican	first known 7 Nov √	.	+
[Hudson] Northern Whig	√	.	+
[Ithaca] American Journal	√	.	+

NEW YORK continued	1820		
[Ithaca] Republican Chronicle	from 6 Sept √	.	+
[Johnstown] Montgomery Monitor	o	.	+
[Johnstown] Montgomery Republican	o	.	+
[Kingston] Craftsman	from 29 Mar √	.	+
[Kingston] Ulster Gazette	x	.	+
[Kingston] Ulster Plebeian	√	.	+
Lansingburgh Gazette	x	.	+
[Malone] Franklin Telegraph	first known 5 Oct x	.	+
[Mayville] Chautauque Eagle	last known 4 Apr √	.	+
[Morrisville] Madison County Gazette	x	.	+
[Moscow] Genesee Farmer	o	.	+
[Mount Pleasant] Westchester Herald	√	.	+
New-York Advertiser	√	.	+
[New York] American	√	.	+
[New York] Columbian	√	.	+
[New York] Commercial Advertiser	√	.	+
New-York Daily Advertiser	√	.	+
New-York Evening Post	√	.	+
New-York Gazette	√	.	+
[New York] Mercantile Advertiser	√	.	+
New-York Messenger	only other known 21 Jan	.	+
[New York] National Advocate	√	.	+
[New York] Patron of Industry	from 28 June √	.	+

Table for 1820

SYMBOLS: √ complete or extensive coverage exists
o no copies extant

× few numbers known (usually less than 25 % of those issued)
+ continued publication after 1820

Chronological Tables of American Newspapers 1690–1820

NEW YORK continued	1820		
New-York Shipping and Commercial List	✓	:	+
[New York] Spectator	✓	:	+
[New York] Weekly Visitor	✓	:	+
[New York] Wood's N.Y. Sale Report	first & only other known: 5 & 19 Feb	:	+
[Newburgh] Political Index	✓	:	+
[Newtown] Investigator	first known 17 June ×	:	+
Norwich Journal	✓	:	+
[Norwich] Republican Agriculturalist	✓	:	+
[Ogdensburgh] St. Lawrence Gazette	○	:	+
[Onondaga] Gazette	○	:	+
Onondaga Register	✓	:	+
Oswego Palladium	✓	:	+
Owego Gazette	×	:	+
Oxford Gazette	✓	:	+
Palmyra Register	✓	:	+
[Peekskill] Westchester Gazette	○	:	+
Penn-Yan Herald	×	:	+
[Plattsburgh] Republican	✓	:	+
Potsdam Gazette	○	:	+
[Poughkeepsie] Dutchess Observer	✓	:	+
Poughkeepsie Journal	✓	:	+
[Poughkeepsie] Republican Herald	×	:	+
Rochester Gazette	resumed 18 Apr ✓	:	+

NEW YORK continued	1820		
Rochester Telegraph	✓	:	+
Sacket's Harbor Gazette	✓	:	+
[Sag Harbor] American Eagle	×	:	+
[Salem] Northern Post	✓	:	+
[Salem] Washington Register	✓	:	+
[Sandy Hill] Times	○	:	+
[Sangerfield] Civil & Religious Intelligencer	○	:	+
[Saratoga Springs] Saratoga Sentinel	✓	:	+
[Schenectady] Cabinet	✓	:	+
[Schoharie] Observer	×	:	+
[Troy] Farmers' Register	×	:	+
[Troy] Northern Budget	✓	:	+
Troy Post	✓	:	+
[Utica] Columbian Gazette	✓	:	+
Utica Observer	○	:	+
[Utica] Patriot	✓	:	+
Waterloo Gazette	✓	:	+
[Watertown] Independent Republican	×	:	+
NORTH CAROLINA			
Edenton Gazette	✓	:	+
[Fayetteville] Carolina Observer	○	:	+
Fayetteville Gazette	only known 22 Nov	:	
Halifax Compiler	○	:	+

NORTH CAROLINA continued	1820	
Hillsborough Recorder	first known 1 Mar √	+
[New Bern] Carolina Centinel	. √	+
[Raleigh] Minerva	. √	+
Raleigh Register	. √	+
[Raleigh] Star	. √	+
[Salisbury] Western Carolinian	from 13 June √	+
[Washington] American Recorder	. ×	+
[Wilmington] Cape-Fear Recorder	. ×	+
OHIO		
[Canton] Ohio Repository	. √	+
[Chillicothe] Scioto Gazette	. √	+
[Chillicothe] Supporter	. √	+
[Chillicothe] Weekly Recorder	. √	+
[Cincinnati] Inquisitor	. √	+
[Cincinnati] Liberty Hall	. √	+
[Cincinnati] Literary Cadet	to 27 Apr √	+
[Cincinnati] Western Spy	. √	+
[Circleville] Olive Branch	. ×	+
Cleaveland Herald	. √	+
Cleaveland Register	to 7 Mar √	+
Columbus Gazette	. √	+
[Columbus] Ohio Monitor	. √	+
[Dayton] Ohio Watchman	. √	+

OHIO continued	1820	
Delaware Gazette	o	+
[Gallipolis] Gallia Gazette	√	+
Hamilton Gazette	√	+
Hillsborough Gazette	√	+
[Lancaster] Ohio Eagle	×	+
[Lebanon] Western Star	√	+
[Marietta] American Friend	resumed 28 Jan √	+
[Mount Pleasant] Philanthropist	√	+
[New Lisbon] Ohio Patriot	√	+
Piqua Gazette	first known 27 July ×	+
[Portsmouth] Scioto Telegraph	from 4 Mar √	+
[Springfield] Farmer	o	+
[Steubenville] Western Herald	√	+
[Troy] Miami Weekly Post	first known 15 June ×	+
[Warren] Western Reserve Chronicle	√	+
[West Union] Political Censor	√	+
[Wooster] Ohio Spectator	×	+
[Worthington] Columbian Advocate	from 7 Jan √	+
[Xenia] Reading Room	last known 10 Aug √	+
Zanesville Express	√	+
[Zanesville] Muskingum Messenger	√	+
PENNSYLVANIA		
[Allentown] Friedens-Bothe	√	+

Table for 1820

SYMBOLS: √ complete or extensive coverage exists
o no copies extant
× few numbers known (usually less than 25% of those issued)
+ continued publication after 1820

Chronological Tables of American Newspapers 1690–1820

PENNSYLVANIA continued	1820	
[Allentown] Unabhängige Republikaner	√	+
Bedford Gazette	×	+
[Bedford] True American	×	+
Bellefonte Patriot	×	+
[Bethany] Wayne County Mirror	o	+
[Brownsville] Western Register	×	+
Butler Centinel	from 7 Oct √	+
[Carlisle] American Volunteer	√	+
Carlisle Herald	×	+
Carlisle Republican	last known 31 Oct √	
Carlisle Whig	first known 15 Mar ×	+
[Chambersburg] Franklin Repository	√	+
[Chambersburg] Franklin Republican	o	+
[Downingtown] American Republican	√	+
[Doylestown] Bucks County Messenger	√	+
Doylestown Democrat	suspended 27 Sept √	+
[Doylestown] Pennsylvania Correspondent	√	+
Easton Centinel	√	+
[Easton] Mountaineer	from 7 Jan √	+
[Easton] Northampton Correspondent	√	+
[Easton] Spirit of Pennsylvania	√	+
[Ebensburg] Olive Branch	only known 17 Feb	
Erie Gazette	first known 22 Jan √	+

Table for 1820

PENNSYLVANIA continued	1820	
Erie Reflector	first & only : / other known : / 20 Mar & 3 Apr .	
[Gettysburg] Adams Centinel	√	+
[Gettysburg] Republican Compiler	√	+
Greensburgh Gazette	√	+
[Greensburg] Westmoreland Republican	√	+
Hannover Gazette	o	+
Hanover Guardian	√	+
[Harrisburg] Chronicle	√	+
Harrisburger Morgenröthe Zeitung	o	+
[Harrisburgh] Oracle of Dauphin	√	+
[Harrisburg] Pennsylvania Intelligencer	from 5 Dec √	+
Harrisburg Republican	to 17 Nov √	+
Huntingdon Gazette	√	+
[Huntingdon] Republican Advocate	from 10 Aug √	+
[Indiana] American	×	+
[Lancaster] Americanische Staatsbothe	×	+
[Lancaster] Free Press	√	+
[Lancaster] Intelligencer	√	+
Lancaster Journal	√	+
[Lancaster] Pennsylvania Gazette	×	+
[Lancaster] Stimme des Volks	first known 2 Sept ×	+
[Lancaster] Volksfreund	×	+
[Lancaster] Wahre Amerikaner	×	+

SYMBOLS: √ complete or extensive coverage exists   × few numbers known (usually less than 25% of those issued)

o no copies extant   + continued publication after 1820

Table for 1820

Chronological Tables of American Newspapers 1690–1820

PENNSYLVANIA continued	1820	
[Williamsport] Lycoming Gazette	×	+
York Gazette	✓	+
York Recorder	✓	+
[York] Wahre Republicaner	○	+
RHODE ISLAND		
Newport Mercury	✓	+
[Newport] Rhode-Island Republican	✓	+
Providence Gazette	✓	+
[Providence] Manufacturers' & Farmers' J.	from 3 Jan ✓	+
Providence Patriot	✓	+
[Providence] Religious Intelligencer	from 13 May to 4 Nov ✓	
[Providence] Rhode-Island American	✓	+
SOUTH CAROLINA		
Camden Gazette	✓	+
[Charleston] Carolina Gazette	✓	+
[Charleston] City Gazette	✓	+
Charleston Courier	✓	+
[Charleston] So. Evangelical Intelligencer	✓	+
[Charleston] Southern Patriot	✓	+
[Charleston] Times	×	+
[Columbia] State Gazette	×	+
[Columbia] Telescope	×	+
[Georgetown] Winyaw Intelligencer	×	+

Table for 1820

SOUTH CAROLINA continued	1820	
[Pendleton] Miller's Weekly Messenger	✓	+
TENNESSEE		
Clarksville Gazette	✓	+
[Jonesborough] East-Tennessee Patriot	×	+
Knoxville Register	✓	+
[Nashville] Clarion	✓	+
Nashville Gazette	✓	+
Nashville Whig	✓	+
[Shelbyville] Tennessee Herald	last known 8 Mar ×	
Sparta Gazette	only known 24 Aug	
VERMONT		
[Bellows Falls] Vermont Intelligencer	✓	+
[Bennington] Vermont Gazette	✓	+
[Brattleboro] Reporter	×	+
[Burlington] Vermont Centinel	×	+
[Danville] North Star	✓	+
[Middlebury] National Standard	✓	+
[Middlebury] Religious Reporter	from 8 Apr; last known 23 Sept ✓	
[Montpelier] Watchman	×	+
Rutland Herald	✓	+
[Windsor] Vermont Journal	✓	+
[Windsor] Vermont Republican	✓	+
Woodstock Observer	from 11 Jan ✓	+

VIRGINIA	1820		
[Abingdon] Political Prospect	o	:	+
[Alexandria] Alexandrian	from 16 Nov √	:	+
[Alexandria] Columbian Telescope	to 20 May √	:	
[Alexandria] Gazette	√	:	+
[Alexandria] Herald	√	:	+
[Charlottesville] Central Gazette	from 29 Jan √	:	+
[Fredericksburg] Virginia Herald	√	:	+
[Leesburg] Genius of Liberty	√	:	+
[Leesburg] Washingtonian	o	:	+
Lexington News-Letter	last known 20 May √	:	
Lynchburg Press	√	:	+
[Norfolk] American Beacon	√	:	+
Norfolk Herald	√	:	+
Petersburg Intelligencer	×	:	+
[Petersburg] Republican	√	:	+
[Richmond] Daily Compiler	√	:	+

VIRGINIA continued	1820		
[Richmond] Enquirer	√	:	+
[Richmond] Virginia Patriot	√	:	+
[Staunton] Republican Farmer	o	:	+
[Warrenton] Palladium of Liberty	√	:	+
[Winchester] Republican Constellation	o	:	+
[Winchester] Virginia Centinel	×	:	+
Woodstock Herald	√	:	+
WEST VIRGINIA			
[Charleston] Kenhawa Spectator	first known 11 Nov ×	:	+
[Charlestown] Farmer's Repository	√	:	+
[Clarksburg] Independent Virginian	×	:	+
[Clarksburg] Republican Compiler	first known 14 Jan; to 28 July √	:	
Martinsburgh Gazette	o	:	+
[Shepherdstown] Informer	only known 12 July	:	
Wellsburgh Gazette	o	:	+
[Wheeling] Va. North-Western Gazette	√	:	+

SYMBOLS: √ complete or extensive coverage exists
o no copies extant

× few numbers known (usually less than 25 % of those issued)
+ continued publication after 1820

Table for 1820